When Kindness Blooms

52 stories to inspire you

DR. STEVEN A. JIRGAL

Published by The Core Media Group, Inc., P.O. Box 2037, Indian Trail, NC 28079.

Printed in the United States of America.

To my wife Pam, a woman who is quick to run to a friend in need—quick to clean a friend's house—quick to invite others in—and quick to allow kindness to bloom in her life.

TABLE OF CONTENTS

INTRODUCTION

Kindness is like a flower that blooms. You don't have to know its name, nor do you have to be the one who planted it, to enjoy the beauty that it brings to your eyes and the delight to your sense of smell.

It may start out as a bulb or a seed. Soon it becomes a sprout and then a stem. Left to its own the stem sends forth a bud that opens, revealing a beautiful flower.

Following is a series of *52 flowers* that have bloomed in someone's life. Many of the stories are based on actual events while others are borne from points of imagination. But each story shares an example of kindness.

Because we are the summation of who we meet, what we experience, and the information we gain, it is hoped that each story will motivate the reader to engage in intentional acts of kindness and develop a heart that naturally chooses kindness when opportunities present themselves.

Like a flower, kindness leaves its' fragrance on every person it touches and its beauty in every eye that sees it. The fragrance it sends forth lingers on the hands that touch it and the beauty of its colors become a part of the memory.

With 52 flowers before you, perhaps you can start your week with the motivational scent and beauty of love and kindness in bloom.

-1-
THE CORRECT SCOREBOARD

Tonight was the night that Steele had been waiting for all season. Tonight, his fourth-grade basketball team would be playing the fifth graders during half time of the varsity game. It was understood that the game would only be a few minutes, but in that short time, Steele and his friends would be cheered on by the gathered masses. As far as he knew, no fourth graders had ever beaten a fifth-grade team and in his young mind, a victory would solidify his team's place in elementary school history. The game occupied his thoughts throughout the day, and he found himself struggling to think of anything else.

The first half of the varsity game seemed to take forever. Steele kept looking at the scoreboard with no interest in the score. His mind was focused on the clock and nothing else. With just two minutes remaining in the first half, his coach ushered the team to a spot behind the bleachers. Nervous energy encircled the boys as their coach went over a few key points and gave some quick words of encouragement. The coach recognized that a pep talk was completely unnecessary, so he instructed the boys to do their best and go out and have fun.

Then the buzzer sounded. Steele could hardly feel his feet touch the floor, as he and his boys jogged to the court. The possibility of making a new mark in history brought their adrenalin juices to new levels. Two of the three officials left the gym while one remained to oversee the contest. The players from each team were introduced and cheers were heard beyond the walls of the gym.

The fifth graders won the tip-off but turned the ball over on a double-dribble. Steele's team inbounded the ball and moved quickly down the court. After a few passes, a shot was missed, and the older kids had the ball once again. A missed shot gave the ball back to the fourth graders and moments later Steele launched one toward the basket. The ball careened to the side, but Steele was fouled in making the attempt. He went to the line with the opportunity to make a second shot if he was successful with the first.

A deep breath and two bounces later, found Steele sending one up and through the hoop. His team was now winning 1-0. History was in the making! His second shot however, missed to the right and a scramble for the ball ensued.

Several players from each team had a chance of possession but Steele came away with the ball. He dribbled several times and found himself in shooting position. He put the ball up and it rounded the hoop three times before dropping in. The roar of the crowd was only overcome by the sound of the buzzer. The game was over and Steele was elated. He knew that he could be seen as nothing other than the hero of the game.

His ecstasy drained when he looked up at the scoreboard and saw that the fifth graders had won 2-1. Within moments he realized what had happened. Somehow, in the battle for the ball, he had gotten twisted around and shot at the wrong basket. He had scored for the other team! The clamor of the crowd was motivated by the victory of the fifth graders! His heart sank and his chin met his chest as he looked for a place to hide. The world became a blur and he wondered if it was possible to recover from such a disaster.

Then above the noise of the crowd he heard a distinct voice. It was a voice that he had heard so many times in his life. It was unmistakable. It was the thundering voice of his father. He looked in the direction of his parents and saw his dad standing up and heard his father yelling over and over again these prideful words with all his might, "THAT'S MY BOY! THAT'S MY BOY! THAT'S MY BOY!!!"

And in that moment, Steele realized that there was more to life than the scoreboard. He knew he had lost the game, but he also knew that in time he would recover. The thundering voice of his dad told him that winning or losing, he would always have his father's heart.

(Adapted from a true story told by Steele Harmon.)

-2-
A HISTORY OF KINDNESS

Eddie stood before the crowd. He wasn't used to speaking in public and he was experiencing more than his share of nerves. But tonight was a night he wouldn't trade for the world. Before him sat many of the most prominent people from the town of Luxley.

The crowd had assembled to honor a member of their own. Tonight was the night they would present the "Man of the year" award to Jake Thomas. Jake was known for taking care of those who couldn't take care of themselves. He volunteered at the local addiction recovery center. He headed the after-school program for underprivileged kids. And every Thanksgiving and Christmas he organized a massive dinner for the homeless. He was a champion of those who struggled.

So, it was very appropriate that he would be receiving this honor and none of those in attendance were the least bit surprised. The award simply followed his reputation. After several announcements, some smaller awards given, and a song presented by four students from the local middle school, Eddie was called to speak on behalf of his friend Jake.

He started by relating his first encounter with Jake. Both boys were freshmen at the local high school. Neither one was a standout athlete nor were they a threat to the valedictorian position. They were simply young men who were meandering their way through school and life.

But somehow Eddie had gotten on the bad side of a few of the older kids in school. It was not uncommon for him to be bumped into his locker from the passing shoulder of one of these bullies. His lunch tray was knocked to the floor more than once, and several times his hat was snatched off his head and flung through an open window. Yet in the midst of all the bullying, Eddie never responded. He felt that to press back against these boys would only bring bigger and more frequent episodes.

Eddie shared with the crowd how at one point his books were knocked out of his hands and kicked across the hall. The boys laughed, called him a name, and moved on. Eddie was on his knees gathering everything up when he bumped into Jake kneeling beside him. Jake helped Eddie collect his books and papers then extended his hand to help him up. Eddie offered a half smile and a quiet thank you.

"Then he said to me something that I'll never forget. He smiled at me and simply said, 'Just remember, not all donkeys live outside.' Then he patted me on the shoulder and said, 'Shake it off. Someday those guys will grow up.' "Then he walked away."

Eddie told the crowd that somehow, he and Jake kept running into each other at school and soon began spending time together on the weekends. They double dated, went on hikes together, and one summer started a lawn care business. In short, they became good friends.

"But no matter where we went, it always seemed like Jake was taking time out to help someone. Loading groceries, bringing home a lost dog, or helping an elderly person into their car are all just part of Jake's DNA. He simply can't help it. He naturally comes to the side of anyone who needs him."

"So, this honor is no surprise. This is given to a Jake Thomas- a man who can't resist the opportunity to help anyone within his reach. Ladies and Gentlemen, I present to you Luxley's man of the year, Mr. Jake Thomas."

The crowd rose to its feet and the room resounded with applause as Jake stood receiving a hug from his wife and a pat on the back from all he passed as he made his way up to the podium.

Eddie met his old friend with a hug and a handshake. When he looked down at Jake's hand, he noticed that he had made an effort to wash it, but it still carried the stains made by an encounter with grease. He didn't ask. He didn't have to. He knew his friend well enough to know that Jake had stopped on his way to the banquet to help someone with car trouble. The juices from his DNA had left their stains on his helping hands.

-3-
LOVE FINDS A WAY

Poor was not an appropriate description of Bill's financial state. In fact, it would take quite a bit of money for him to reach a level where he could be labeled poor. The depression had hit the entire world, but it seemed to hit the Curtis family even harder.

Bill was nineteen and lived with his mother and his father. His dad had been bedridden for two years after a fall from a ladder left him paralyzed from the waist down. Their small farm on the Georgia-Alabama border was anything but productive. Bill and his mother Nora toiled endlessly to make it work but a drought had ruined their crops and a virus had cut the livestock in half. Hard work and a strong commitment to the family had made Bill as strong on the inside as he was on the outside.

Though he had so little, Bill held two possessions close to his heart. One was his dog named Sarge. He was a such a mixture of breeds that one could only guess his heritage. He was a medium sized dog with short hair and long ears. His black fur was splotched with white dots and the markings on his head and face were a random blend of spots and lines. Sarge was as loyal as he was wild. He lived in the barn but was found by Bill's side the moment he left the house. Bill and Sarge traversed the farm together and numerous times Sarge could be heard growling at some foreign four-legged intruder in protection of Bill. Though Sarge never left Bill's side, he also never left the farm. If Bill headed to town or left for an errand, Sarge would walk him to the dirt road and head back to the barn. When Bill returned, Sarge returned to the edge of the property and welcomed him back.

Bill's other possession was his belt. It was given to him by his grandfather shortly before he passed away and was the center of Bill's pride. It carried a good-sized gold-plated buckle with a thick strap made of genuine bison leather. Bill donned his belt wherever he went with the buckle leading the way and catching everyone's eye.

But as poor as Bill was in material things, he was rich in his love for Audrey. She had captured his heart in high school and the two had deepened their affections over the past two years.

Audrey was as kind as she was beautiful. She too was an only child and spent much of her free time helping the family at their small grocery store in town. Her slender build and long golden hair complimented her deep blue eyes, and her laughter filled any room with smiles and nods of approval. She had a winsome personality, and it came as no surprise that Bill would be drawn to her.

Whenever time permitted, the two would slip off to enjoy some much-needed relief from their demanding roles in their families. Walks in the park, star gazing, sandwiches in the barn were always accompanied by their dreams of how life would someday be better when there were no goodbyes attached to the end of their day. The plan was that they would marry and live on the lower end of the farm. There was a large shed there and Bill would often escort Audrey there and share his ideas on converting it to a small home. There would only be room for one bedroom, but they were both convinced that their love would enlarge the little house and turn it into a darling home.

One sunny Sunday afternoon, as Bill and Audrey walked back from church, Bill slipped his hand in Audrey's and asked her a question that was heavy on his mind. "Audrey" he said as he turned to her, "What's keeping us from getting married now? What are we waiting for?" Audrey was not ready for that question, but it immediately started her wheels turning. She returned his gaze and her smile revealed that she had no solid objection. Each lover knew that their parents approved, and they had often shared how their parents would bring up the marital subject.

So, the plan was set. On Friday, Bill and Audrey would meet at the edge of town in the early evening. He had shared with her that the county line was only two miles away and the cost of a marriage license in Howard County was only $1.00-a good bit cheaper than in their home county.

The week crept by. In the middle of the week the two met at Audrey's house and solidified their plans while enjoying a glass of iced tea on the front porch swing. Containing their excitement became a focal point of the remainder of the week. If it were possible, they felt that their love for one another grew as the reality of their marriage came into view. Would Friday ever arrive?

Friday did come and just like the week, it moved painfully slow. Finally, the time came for the two to leave their respective positions and head for the edge of town. At the store, Audrey slipped out the door informing her mother that Bill needed her help with something. She was gone before her mother had a chance to reply or protest. She whisked her way back home and quickly put on a dress. Bill changed clothes in the barn and simply disappeared from the farm.

Bill arrived first at the feed store on the edge of town. He spent the entire time targeting his eyes down the street to get a glimpse of his love. Minutes later she appeared and the passion of their kiss and embrace brought stares and smiles from those passing by. Hand in hand they walked to the magistrate's home in Howard County.

The magistrate opened the door on the first knock. He was accustomed to couples coming to his home and knew what they wanted before they got a chance to explain. They were handed papers and in a flash Bill's heart sank. Without saying a word, he pointed to the fee for a license-$2.00. He wasn't sure if he misheard, or the price had gone up. What he did know was he only had $1.00 .25 cents of which was borrowed from his cousin. Audrey went numb. They asked if they could pay later and were informed that it was a violation of the law not to pay in full at the time of the licensing. They both sat down and hung their heads in disbelief.

Then Bill's face shot up. He had an idea. "Wait here! I'll be right back." With that he bolted through the door and ran toward town. A few minutes later Bill returned with one hand holding a dollar and the other holding his pants up. He explained that he had gone to the bar and sold his leather belt to the bartender. The great sacrifice registered on Audrey's face and her heart soared.

After handing the magistrate the money, two witnesses were summoned from the other room and moments later Bill and Audrey were declared husband and wife.

Barely touching the ground, the pair worked their way back home with Bill struggling the entire way to hold his pants up. After sharing the news with Audrey's parents, they spent the night with Bill's family.

The next evening both sets of parents dined at the Curtis' home in celebration of their union. Somehow food was in abundance with the meal being topped off by a large chocolate cake bearing their names. The evening was completed when Bill was presented with a gift from Audrey's parents. Bill's heart skipped a beat as he opened the box and discovered his precious belt. The evening was completed with laughter and great cheer with both families understanding that love always makes a way.

-4-
LOVE'S REACTION

Lance and Michelle wore their ten years of marriage as a badge of honor. They had three children under the age of six and displayed continual love for their little ones. Protection and provision were the benchmarks of the couple's relationship.

He was a supervisor at the truck mill and brought home a consistent paycheck. He worked at the mill for over nine years and held pride in the fact that he had never missed a day and was never late. His coworkers held him in high regard and saw him as a fair and honest leader. Going without was commonplace for Lance. He intentionally gave up what he wanted so he could give his family what they needed and often wanted, and Michelle never missed acknowledging and appreciating it.

Lance also protected the family physically by stepping into harm's way when necessary and never let a night go by when he didn't secure the doors to their little home. If one were to follow the family when out for a walk you would always find Lance on the *Car side,* or the *Dog side* of the sidewalk whichever posed the most danger.

Michelle had her way of providing and protecting the family as well. She was a wonderful cook providing meals that were both nutritious and delicious. By shopping during sales days, their children were always warm in the winter and cool in the summer. She taught the children and led them in making crafts and artwork. They sang songs, went to the park, read stories, and built bedroom forts together. She knew they didn't have many extras but saw the value in building memories rather than monuments.

One cold winter Saturday morning, the family awoke to find twelve inches of fresh snow on the ground. The weather began to warm and Lance and Michelle knew that a romp in the snow would be short lived. After breakfast, the entire family went for a long walk. Michelle had wrapped each of the children from head to toe ensuring their warmth and protection. She carried the smallest one on her back, and off they went into the white fabric of the season. Snowmen, snow angels, and snowballs were all part of the adventure.

The family circled a large field and worked their way through the woods. Exiting the other side brought them out to the road. When a few complaints of the cold were issued they began to make their way back to the house. They were walking along the front of a store when they heard a loud and strange noise above them. Looking up, they all saw a large sheet of water laden snow sliding off the metal roof. Without hesitation, Lance pushed the entire family into the street knocking two of the children off their feet. There was no room or time for him to get out of the way and he absorbed the full impact of the slushy avalanche.

The force of the wet snow drove Lance to the ground and his cheek bone bounced off the sidewalk. The wind was knocked out of him and instantly he was drenched in the icy water. A shiver ran up his spine as he struggled to catch his breath and sit up. He couldn't decide which was greater, the cold or the dizziness.

Within seconds, Michelle and the kids were helping Lance to his feet.

The family walked home slowly with Michelle walking with her arm around Lance's waist and the children walking on his other side. When they reached the house, Michelle rushed to the bathroom and filled the tub with warm water. Just minutes later Lance was enjoying the return of his normal body temperature and the relief brought on by an ice pack on his cheek.

When Lance emerged from the tub, he was clad in a bathrobe and slippers. The children escorted him to his easy chair where he found a warm blanket Michelle had just pulled from the dryer. He climbed under the blanket and was soon joined by the two older children. A minute later Michelle handed him their youngest child and a warm mug of hot cocoa.

And as the children snuggled with him under the blanket, Lance gave a heavy and satisfying sigh and thought, "Protection and provision, looks like it runs in the family!"

-5-
THE SHINE OF CARING

Everything seemed so surreal to Abbey. Things were going so well with their family. Mark had a new job, their four young children were enjoying life, and the town they moved to seemed pleasant and accepting. They had even found a church that all six of them enjoyed and looked forward to attending.

Then the report from the doctor came. Cancer! Again! Mark had beaten lung cancer once about three years ago and was doing well and feeling good. After six months of chemotherapy and radiation, they removed a small portion of his left lung. He recovered quickly and life was normal and good again.

But four months ago, the doctor called them in to give them the terrifying news. The cancer had returned with a vengeance and there was nothing they could do past the point of keeping him comfortable. Pods of cancer were found in both lungs, and it had spread to his liver and one of his kidneys. Mark and Abbey sat in the doctor's office in silence, staring at the floor.

Those four months went faster than Abbey could ever imagine. They did manage to keep Mark comfortable, and Abbey and the children stayed by his side the entire time. The morning he died he exhibited such peace and shared whispers of encouragement for each of the children. Then he rubbed the back of Abbey's hand gave a half smile, exhaled and was gone.

And now she faced the day when they would lay his body to rest. She had explained things to the children as best she could, and they seemed to have a small level of understanding equal to their age.

They were sad and didn't try to hide it. The tears flowed quickly and often, and they did their best to comfort each other.

And now it was time for them all to get dressed and drive over to the church house for the *Celebration of life* service. Abbey was busy gathering clothes for each of the children and Claire, her oldest pitched in and helped dress each one.

Though she was only seven Claire was bright and mature beyond her age and was constantly finding ways to help. The scramble in the house was interrupted by a knock on the door. Abbey took a deep breath and shook her head in a *Not now* response.

She could see through the sheer curtain on the door that it was Stephen, a neighbor from down the street. He was holding a cake in one hand and had a box pressed under his other arm. Stephen was a quiet man who owned the deli in town. Though he was well over seventy, he was active as a volunteer of the local animal shelter and a member of the Elks club.

Abbey opened the door and was greeted by a nod and a half smile. He pushed the cake toward her and said, "Kathryn made this for you." Abbey smiled and said, "Thank you." She followed this with, "Listen, we're a little busy right now. I'm trying to get the kids ready, and we really don't have time to visit." Stephen smiled, "I didn't come by to visit." Then patting the box he said, "I came to polish the children's shoes. Most kids' shoes are in need of a little shine. Bring them to me and I'll take care of them."

Abbey looked down. Her thankfulness showed through the tears that were shining on her eyes. "Of course. I'll go get them." Moments later Stephen was seated on the front steps putting a finish on each of the children's shoes. When he was on the third pair, he felt the door open behind him. It was Claire. She was dressed in a black skirt with a white top. She stepped over to Stephen and sat down next to him silently watching him work. When he picked up the last pair of shoes, he felt Claire's head gently rest against his shoulder. He pressed his shoulder slightly into her cheek and smiled.

After a few more moments Claire got up, kissed Stephen gently on the side of his forehead and whispered, "Thank you." Stephen fought back the tears and whispered, "You're welcome."

Having finished the task, Stephen put his supplies away and

placed the lid on the box. He carried all four pairs of little shoes to the house and placed them just inside the door. Picking up his box, he quietly made his way down the steps.

He turned back toward the house as the door opened behind him. Abbey stood there wearing a black dress and holding the youngest child. "Thank you, Stephen," she said quietly. Stephen placed his hand over his heart, tapped it twice, nodded and walked away.

-6-
THE WINNING SCORE

Fans rooted for the competition. Cheerleaders switched loyalties. The coach helped the opposition score points. Parents yelled for the competition.

What was this?

The scene was birthed by a big-hearted football coach in Grapevine, Texas. Kris Hogan leads the successful program of Faith Christian High School. He has seventy players, eleven coaches, quality equipment, and parents who care, make banners, attend pep rallies, and never miss a game.

They took their 7-2 record into a contest with Gainesville State School. Gainesville's players, by contrast, wear seven-year-old shoulder pads and helmets from a decade ago. They show up at each game wearing handcuffs. Their parents don't watch them play, but twelve uniformed officers do. That's because Gainesville is a maximum-security prison. The school doesn't have a stadium, cheerleading squad, or half a hope of winning. Gainesville was 0-8 going into the Grapevine game. They'd scored two touchdowns all year.

The whole situation didn't seem fair. So, Coach Hogan devised a plan. He asked the fans to step across the field and, for one night only, cheer for the other side. More than two hundred volunteered.

The people formed a forty-yard spirit line. They painted "Go Tornadoes!" on a banner that the Gainesville squad could burst through. They sat on the Gainesville side of the stadium. They even learned the names of Gainesville players so they could yell for individuals.

The prisoners had heard people scream their names but never like this. Gerald, a lineman who will serve three years, said, "People are a little afraid of us when we come to the games. You can see it in their eyes. They're lookin' at us like we're criminals. But these people, they were yellin' FOR us-by our names!"

After the game the teams gathered in the middle of the field to say a prayer. One of the incarcerated players asked to lead it. Coach Hogan agreed, not knowing what to expect. "Lord," the boy said, "I don't know how this happened, so I don't know how to say thank you, but I never would've known there was so many people in the world that cared about us."

Grapevine fans weren't finished. After the game they waited beside the Gainesville bus to give each player a good-bye gift-burger, fries, candy, soda, a Bible, an encouraging letter, and a round of applause. As their prison bus left the parking lot, the players pressed stunned faces against the windows and wondered what had just hit them.

(Adapted from an article written by Rick Reilly-ESPN)

-7-
A SONG IN THE NIGHT

The university entrance interview was just one week away, and Sam was feeling all the pressure any eighteen-year-old could bear. All his life, he dreamed of attending Warren University but to gain entrance to the music program, he had to write and perform a short piece.

Music was Sam's life. He loved it and he lived it. He had taught himself to play the guitar, the piano, and the trumpet. He didn't write music and he struggled while reading it, but if a tune was in the air, Sam could capture it and perform it identically as it was played. He had a gift, and he was looking forward to developing it and Warren University was just the place to take him to *the next level*. He had dreams of leading a band, performing solos, and teaching music. He knew he needed to learn to read music and he was eager to jump in with total commitment. But he needed to come up with both the words and music to an original piece.

Sam belonged to a small band and each of the guys tried to help him along. But somehow things were not coming together, and Sam was certain that he hadn't come up with anything worthy of getting him into the school. Each time he thought he was headed in the right direction, a tune that he was very familiar with would invade his mind and he found himself transitioning into the well-known song.

Frustration and panic were racing to take control of his mind and he began to doubt that he had what it takes to get into the school much less succeed as a student. Fortunately, Sam's grandparents were celebrating their 65th wedding anniversary and Sam was looking forward to the distraction.

When Sam and his parents arrived at the banquet hall the place was filled with friends and family. His Grandma and Grandpa were seated at the head table and a continual stream of well-wishers came by. Sam and his folks found a table and enjoyed a visit with some friends. Soon, dessert was served, and everyone indulged and continued enjoying the evening. Sam slipped up to his Grandparent's table and sat with them. The talk was casual and light-hearted, but when Sam stood to return to his table, his Grandpa put his hand on Sam's forearm. He looked Sam in the eye and said, "Sammy, it's coming. Whatever you're looking for, it's coming. Just keep those eyes open and you'll see it!" Then he patted Sam's arm. Sam nodded and gave each of them a hug and turned to rejoin his parents.

Speeches were made, songs were sung, and memories were relived. It was a joyful night and the guests of honor felt loved and cared for. It was not a late night, but it was filled with great fellowship and a deep celebratory spirit.

Back home, Sam watched a little television and then headed for bed. In short order he found himself drifting off to sleep.

Less than an hour later something strange happened. Sam wasn't awake, but he wasn't dreaming either. He was laying on his back when he opened his eyes and stared up at the ceiling. A tune began to swim in his mind. It was a soft tune but carried with it a measure of depth that pulled at Sam's heart.

Sam scrambled out of bed and pulled a pad from his desk. The tune never left his mind but now he could feel words coming out and attaching them to the music. Sam wrote as fast as he could with a growing fear that time would steal the words or tune. But neither the words nor the tune escaped, and Sam captured all the words that fit the music. When he dropped his pen, he gave a heavy sigh and gently shook his head in disbelief. He had it! He had the song that he would be sharing with the music department at Warren University!

TOGETHER STILL
Let me hold your hand as we go downhill,
We've shared our strength and we share it still.

It hasn't been easy to make the climb
But the way was eased by your hand in mine.

Like the lake, our life has had ripples too,
Ill-health, and worries, and payments due,
With happy pauses along the way,
A graduation, a raise in pay.

Let me hold your hand as we go downhill,
We started with love, and we love still.

At the foot of the slope, we will stop and rest,
Look back, if you wish: we've been truly blessed.
We've been spared the grief of being torn apart
By death, or divorce, or a broken heart.

The view ahead is one of the best,
Just a little bit farther, and then we can rest.
We move more slowly, but together still,
Let me hold your hand as we go downhill.

Yes, let me hold your hand as we go downhill,
I loved you then, and I love you still.
Let me hold your hand as we go downhill,
Let me hold your hand, let me hold your hand.

Sam's song was very well received, and he gained admittance to the university. *Together Still* became a campus favorite and Sam was able to sell it to a well-known band. The royalty he received paid for two years of his education and he graduated and began a long career in various aspects of the music world.

And although time marched on, and life tried to crowd it out, he never forgot the touch, or the night his grandfather's assurance came to life.

(*Together Still* was adapted from a poem by Peggy Cameron King)

-8-
KINDNESS GIVES

Modern Maturity notes, "The world is full of two kinds of people, the givers and the takers. The takers eat well, but the givers sleep well."

Annie Jefferson was a giver in the highest sense of the word. She gave to her community. She volunteered at the pregnancy center. She organized an after-school program for kids struggling academically. She served at the Thanksgiving and Christmas dinners for the homeless. She even helped construct and paint the town's welcome center and quite often went without sleep to stay up with a friend in the hospital.

Annie also gave to her family. She made crafts with her three young children and attended every play and special event they had at school. If there was a need they had, she made sure to meet it. When her husband Dean came home from work, there was always a well-prepared meal and a ready smile waiting for him. Every birthday celebration in the Jefferson home was a celebration indeed. Music, presents, food, and cake were in abundance, and the message of love and appreciation for the birthday person was more than apparent. Annie was a giver, and she always gave time, energy, resources, and love.

One Thursday night, the elementary school held an *Open House* night. Annie not only attended, but brought cookies for each class her two older children were in. She visited each teacher and got an update on how each of them was doing. It came as no surprise to Annie that Lisa was doing well in every subject. She had a lot of friends and was well behaved. She had a similar report from Matthew's teacher which she expected.

The school was almost empty when Annie came to Mrs. Dunn's third grade class. The two ladies were alone, and Annie was slightly surprised when she was greeted with a firm and unexpected hug. It wasn't just a *hello* type of hug. It was more on the level of a *I am so thankful for you* embrace.

Mrs. Dunn led Annie to a chair and the two ladies sat down. The teacher shared how Dean was a good student and was doing well in all his subjects. She noted that he was very energetic and talkative, and his name was put in the *Yellow Zone* a couple of times. He always adjusted his behavior and never made it to the *Red Zone*. None of this information was news to Annie. She nodded and explained that Dean acted that way at home as well.

Mrs. Dunn shared with her an episode in class involving Dean. The students were just beginning a session on fractions.

"Everyone seemed to do well and followed the concept."

Annie nodded.

"Then I gave examples to each of the children and asked them for an answer."

Annie seemed puzzled but remained silent.

"I asked Dean, 'suppose your mother made a cake. There are seven of you in the family. Your mom, dad, and uncle, and aunt, and you three kids. When she cut the cake into equal parts, what part of the cake would you get?'"

Annie had no idea where this was going but leaned forward to make sure she understood.

The teacher continued, "Dean said, 'One sixth.'"

Annie was surprised and guessed that Dean simply didn't understand the scenario.

"I repeated the question, and he came up with the same answer. I was somewhat frustrated and posed the question a third time. But Dean insisted on the same answer."

Annie was visibly surprised and confused. Dean had always done well in math and his teacher had said everyone seemed to be grasping the concept.

Mrs. Dunn continued, "I asked Dean if he didn't understand the question and he said, 'I know the question. But I also know my mother. She'd say she didn't want any cake.'"

Annie blushed a bit and gave a broad smile and a small sigh of relief.

Mrs. Dunn stood, and Annie joined her. "Your son is doing fine Mrs. Jefferson, and so are you!"

And a grin remained glued to Annie's face the entire ride home.

-9-
TIME FOR FRIENDSHIP

Geoffrey loved to run. Distance running was part of his life. He came from a family of runners. His two brothers were runners. His father had been a runner. Even his uncle had completed a few marathons. So, it was natural that running road races became his way of keeping the pounds off, staying in shape, and enjoying the challenges of racing. He had run several different types of races including 5k's (3.1 miles), 10k's (6.2 miles), half marathons (13.1 miles), and the 26.2-mile marathon.

Geoffrey loved getting out early in the morning, just as the sun was poking its eye over the mountaintops. Cold air, rain, and even a bit of snow did not detract him from getting in his morning run. Mountain runs, wooded runs, and runs along isolated country roads were his favorite venues for his longer treks.

Geoffrey competed in several races each year. Some were longer than others, but one race in particular called him back year after year. It was the Keystone marathon. He had run it more than five times and with each effort his time was better than the last. It became the race that demonstrated his progress and he used it as a benchmark for improvement. The race took place in Mechanicsburg Pa. and was a healthy mixture of hills and flats. Part of the race brought the runners along the Susquehanna River with several views of the city of Harrisburg.

In three weeks, the Keystone Marathon would take place and Geoffrey felt more prepared than ever. The usual foot issues and nagging back pains didn't show up and Geoffrey felt no need to back off the intensity of his work outs. He had pushed himself hard for it and was sure that this year his time and place would be better than ever. His enthusiasm grew as the calendar turned toward the day of the race.

Geoffrey worked as a CPA in a large firm in Virginia. He was able to take that Friday off and used it to travel from his home outside of Richmond to Pennsylvania. He stayed in the same hotel and ate at the same restaurant each time he showed up to compete.

He rested well that Friday night and rose early to head to the fairgrounds for the start of the race. While driving he drank a quart of water and ate two protein bars. As in other years, the number of runners was large but for some reason Geoffrey thought this was the largest ever. As he milled around the other athletes, he came across a co-worker named Don. Neither of them knew the other was competing and both were surprised by the encounter. Geoffrey didn't know Don well but remembered someone telling him how much of an accomplished runner Don was. While they were talking, he learned that Don's best marathon time was several minutes faster than his own. The men agreed to run together and as the gun went off, they ran side by side with the swarm of other runners.

Geoffrey felt good, took in fluids as he went, and was encouraged that although the pace was fast, he was able to keep up with Don. After five miles Geoffrey was still striding strongly and was several minutes ahead of his target time.

At the ten-mile mark, he felt himself dragging a bit but still managed to run with Don. He felt no leg cramps and knew that the hard work he had done was paying off.

When they eclipsed fifteen miles, Geoffrey began to think that the pace was a little too strong for him and a couple of miles later he backed off a bit. Don charged on ahead, but Geoffrey was able to keep him in sight.

After running for twenty miles, Geoffrey felt the strain of the race. He kept taking in fluids but knew that the race was taking its toll on his body. He was still significantly ahead of his target time, but knew he had to slow down even more if he was to finish the race.

With just two miles to go he knew two things: he was going to finish, and he felt certain he was going to beat his best time. He held the new pace he had established and focused on putting one foot in front of the other. His legs felt so heavy, and he sensed a little burning in his lungs. A couple of times he felt a spasm in his left hamstring and feared that a cramp was coming on. But the finish line was now just a half-mile away and he pressed ahead with everything he had.

At the end of a long and straight road, he could see the banner over the finish line. The crowd had swelled to gigantic proportions and the noise they made was both deafening and encouraging.

It was then that he saw Don. He was on the side of the road bent over with his hands on his knees. The blood running down his shin gave evidence of a fall. Geoffrey was tempted to drive on to the finish line, but something inside just wouldn't let him continue. He slowed his pace and slid over to the side of the road. He asked if Don was okay and learned that he had a bad cramp in his right calf and couldn't go on.

Once again, Geoffrey had to fight the temptation to finish on his own. "I can help you finish" was all he said. Don looked up and in a heavy breath said, "Yes, finish."

Geoffrey put his arm around Don and helped him limp the final three hundred yards to the finish line. The crowd was going crazy screaming encouragement to the two men. They crossed the line together and Don slid to the ground while workers surrounded him with ice packs, a warming blanket, and electrolyte drinks. Geoffrey grabbed a couple of drinks and began to walk off the fatigue his body was dealing with.

There was a large clock on the side of a building and Geoffrey could tell that he failed to beat his best time by about a minute. Though he failed to reach his goal, and missed the exhilarating feeling of success, he did gain a life-long friend. With little effort, Geoffrey learned that the clock is not the determining factor in winning.

-10-
THE GEM OF LOVE

Tonight was the night Lisa had been waiting for all week. It was her and Steve's tenth wedding anniversary. Tonight, they would go out to her favorite restaurant and eat a wonderful meal and afterwards ride a horse-drawn carriage along the Milton River. It promised to be a night filled with good food, pleasant conversation, the sharing of memories, and a good dose of romance.

As she dressed for the evening, she reflected on their lives together. They had met over a decade earlier when he was a college senior, and she was a junior. They began dating just after Christmas and before long were both very much in love and deeply committed to one another. Steve was a kind man and always looked after her. He provided well for her and their two children and seemed greatly satisfied with family life. Their lives were far from perfect. They struggled with job changes, minor health issues, the funeral of Steve's father, and a few investment disappointments. But when looking at the big picture, they both agreed that they were very blessed. And so here they were, ten years, two children, three moves and three jobs later getting ready to celebrate their ten years together.

Lisa was wearing a beautiful gown and putting on the finishing touches to her hair while waiting for Steve to arrive from work. He wouldn't need much time to get ready and soon they would be off for a memorable evening with the one they loved.

With her earrings already in place, Lisa reached into the second drawer of her jewelry box. There she pulled out a gold necklace with three diamonds hanging from the center. She slipped the necklace on and fastened it in the back on her first try. Immediately her mind spun back to ten years ago, when she had worn a similar one for the first time.

Steve and Lisa were the proverbial couple that was short on money and long on love. During the months leading up to their wedding day, Steve worked as an accountant. To make some extra money for their honeymoon, he had taken a job working for his uncle's package delivery business on the weekends. His sister Regina was a travel agent and had worked some angles allowing them to be able to afford a complete five-night stay at a resort in Jamaica. The wedding was in their local church with the reception in the fellowship hall downstairs.

Their wedding was everything Lisa had dreamed of. The decorations, the music, the bridal party, and the ceremony all came together to make a perfect day and to launch them into a great future.

After the reception, Steve's best man and best friend Thomas pulled him aside for a word in private. He wished them well and then handed Steve a fifty-dollar bill for every day they would be away. It was an unexpected but welcomed blessing to the groom. Then Steve and Lisa quickly changed clothes and headed to a hotel near the airport. After dinner and dessert Steve handed a small box to his new wife. When Lisa opened it, she found the most beautiful gold necklace her young eyes had ever seen. In the center of the chain was a small shiny diamond. Lisa was overwhelmed and through her tears did her best to communicate her love and appreciation for Steve.

The next day they found themselves aboard a plane bound for Jamaica. Life was good and Steve and Lisa knew it.

Jamaica was wonderful! The beach, the restaurants, the suite, and the weather made for a perfect honeymoon. The couple bathed in the love they carried for one another.

But on the fourth evening of their trip something happened that would be etched in their memories forever. Steve and Lisa were out for a moonlight walk on the beach. They were within the property lines of the resort, and felt safe. They stood watching the moon bounce off the waves and never saw a man approaching them from the side. With a native accent he said, "Excuse me sir. Do you have the time?" Steve extended his arm to look at his watch. In an instant the man tore the necklace off Lisa with one hand while his knife slashed the side of her neck with the other. Blood hit Steve in the face as Lisa screamed, grabbed her neck, and fell to her knees. Chasing the man never entered Steve's mind. All his attention went to his bleeding wife.

Lisa was rushed to the hospital where her wounded neck received nineteen sutures. The knife edge had barely missed her carotid artery and she was released shortly after the procedure.

Back at the resort, the couple sat on the edge of the bed recounting what had happened and sharing their thoughts of thankfulness. At one point, Lisa began to cry. Steve assumed that she was in pain and asked her, "Are you hurting?" "No" she replied as she quietly sobbed. "He took my necklace! I can't believe he took my necklace!" Steve gently put his arm around her shoulders and pulled her close to him. "Listen" he said. "I can get another necklace. But there will never be another you!" She smiled and gently kissed his hand.

The next day the two of them were on an afternoon flight for the States. Lisa had minimal pain and the couple were anxious to settle into their new life and marriage. Steve sat next to her asleep and Lisa stared out the window thankful for her husband. Constantly fighting back tears, she kept looking down and touching the new and beautiful necklace the love of her life bought earlier that morning.

The opening of the front door brought Lisa back to the present. Steve made his way up the stairs and in moments was standing in the doorway to their bedroom with an armful of roses. Both Steve and Lisa knew that this night was going to be filled with enough love for three couples. And for the rest of their lives together they were enveloped with love, affection, and thankfulness for each other.

-11-
FRIENDSHIPS PRICE

Curtis and Mike were the best of friends and grew up together in the small town of Daphne, on the edge of Mobile, Alabama. They spent their time attending school together and when not in school, exploring the nearby woods looking for any sign of adventure. They built forts, hunted rabbits, fished, and climbed the tallest of trees. They worked to help their family through the depression and quickly shared any means to turn a dollar. They readily shared their anger as well as their dreams and enjoyed as transparent a relationship as any two young men can.

On more than one occasion, one of the boys found himself in danger of a beating from a group of older kids. The fight did not always go his way, but he never fought alone. His buddy was by his side taking and giving blows with everything he had. Later, they compared bruises and blood marks and bragged about who got the worst of it.

After Mike developed a severe case of bronchitis, Curtis was often found by his bedside, telling him stories, helping him with his medications, and simply being a friend. He brought Mike's schoolwork home and made sure he was comfortable.

As time went on the boys grew to be closer friends with loyalty that surpassed their combined years. Where one was found, the other was never far away. And when one was in trouble, the other was quick to jump in.

When WW II broke out, both boys felt compelled to enlist in the army to defend their country and ensure freedom for the world.

They were both underage but agreed to falsify the papers enabling them to enlist. With great pride they found themselves in basic training.

They went through boot camp side by side offering encouragement and advice and looking out for one another the entire time. In short order they found themselves on the soil of Germany, dodging bullets and fighting the elements.

Month after month they lived out their lives in the trenches, in the cold and the mud, under fire and under orders. From time to time one side or the other would rise up out of the trenches, fling their bodies against the opposing line and slink back to lick their wounds, bury their dead, and wait to do it all over again. In the process, Curtis and Mike's friendship was welding into unbreakable steel. Day after day, night after night, terror after terror, they talked of life, of families, of hopes, of what they would do when (and if) they returned from this horror.

On one more fruitless charge, Curtis fell, severely wounded. Mike made it back to the relative safety of the trenches. Meanwhile Curtis lay suffering beneath the night flares. Between both armies. Alone.

The shelling continued. The danger was at its peak. Between the trenches was no place to be. Still, Mike wished to reach his friend, to comfort him, to offer the encouragement only a friend can give. The officer in charge refused to let Mike leave the trench. It was simply too dangerous. As he turned his back, however, Mike went over the top. Ignoring the smell of cordite in the air, the concussion of incoming rounds, and the pounding in his chest, Mike made it to Curtis.

Sometime later he managed to get Curtis back to the safety of the trenches. But it was too late. His friend was gone. The somewhat self-righteous officer, seeing Curtis' body, cynically asked Mike if it had been "worth the risk." Mike's response was without hesitation.

"Yes, sir, it was," he said. "Curtis' last words made it more than worth it. He looked up at me and said, 'I knew you'd come.'"

(Adapted from "Stories for the Heart"-Stu Weber)

-12-
A STRANGER'S KINDNESS

It was a busy day for Leslie. For an unknown reason, she had gotten little sleep last night. After downing a couple of cups of coffee, she took her seven-year-old grand-son Timothy to Edison elementary school on the other side of town.

She circled back to the house, did two loads of laundry, cleaned both bathrooms, and ironed two arm loads of shirts and pants. When she was finished, she had just enough time to make lunch and take it Timothy's school for *Grandparents Day*.

The second graders sang a song, read a few stories they had written, and took turns solving the math problems on the board. It was a drain on her patience, but Leslie did her best to stay focused on all the things Timothy was showing her in his classroom. School dismissed early that day, so Leslie and Timothy made their way back to his house. A couple of hours later, Timothy's mom came home, and Leslie was free to continue with her overwhelming day.

After getting gas, she dropped off a birthday gift for the pastor's wife and made her way to the grocery store. If things went well at the store, she could be home in time to have dinner ready for her husband Tom when he returned from work.

When Leslie turned her car into the grocery store parking lot, she immediately saw that the store was packed with customers. She circled the lot a couple of times with no luck in finding a place to park. Finally, she found an open space on the back corner of the building.

She made her way to the store pulling out her list as she went. She had several items to purchase and after thirty minutes she was able to join the long line at the checkout counter. Fifteen minutes later she was pushing her cart toward her car behind the store.

She opened her trunk remotely and began filling it with her groceries. She was almost done when she heard a voice behind her. "Hey Ma'am." Leslie turned to find a homeless-looking man standing uncomfortably close to her. His clothes were greatly tattered, and his face was completely covered with grey and black hair. His shoes were beyond the point where they could be labeled worn. She stepped back and felt the open truck behind her. He stepped toward her, pointed at her pocketbook, and in a gravelly voice asked, "Have you got any money you could give me?" Leslie sensed that it was more of a demand than a question and although her heart was racing, she did her best to remain calm.

Leslie reached toward the shopping cart and slowly moved it between her and the man. She was trapped between the man and her car but at least now there was a barrier between her and the stranger. She stammered a reply, "No. I don't carry cash." The man put his hand on the cart and said, "What about some food from your trunk?" Leslie was too startled to look back at her trunk. She dared not take her eyes off the man.

Suddenly she heard a man call out, "Nancy! Hey Nancy!" She turned slightly toward the front of her car and saw a middle-aged man moving toward her on the driver's side. "Good to see you!" The man nodded toward the homeless man while reaching behind Leslie and closing her trunk.

Leslie was speechless. She had never seen this man before and wasn't sure how to react. "Listen" he said as he gave her a wink, "I've got your husband's book in my car. Leslie's face showed a connection with the stranger's words. "Come on over and let me give it to you." With that, he gently took her arm and led her away from the back of her car and the homeless man who never responded.

When the two of them had walked toward the front of the store Leslie finally spoke.

"Thank you! Thank you so much!"

The man smiled and said, "No problem. I saw that you were cornered, and I couldn't think of anything else to do. By the way, my name's Dennis."

"I'm Leslie" She replied. "I was so scared. I never saw him coming. Thank you so much!"

"Glad I could help" he said.

The two of them stood near the front of the store until they saw the homeless man walk away on the other side of the parking lot. "I think it's safe to head back to your car now" Dennis said. "I'll walk you back and make sure you get in." "Thank you for being so kind!" Leslie replied.

At home, Leslie related the entire story to Tom. Tom was captivated by her story and so grateful that a man would come by and rescue her like that. When she finished relating the incident Tom stood up and gave her a strong hug.

Late that night, as Leslie's tired head hit the pillow, she fell asleep while praying, "Lord, thank you for protecting me by sending Dennis my way. Please bless that kind man in a way that he'll know your hand has touched him. With that, she rolled to her side and was quickly sound asleep.

-13-
BLIND FRIENDSHIP

It had been a good day for Allie. She and her husband Brandon had enjoyed a nice date the previous night including pizza and a long walk by the lake. She rested well and was set for a new day as she home-schooled her oldest daughter and looked after the two younger boys. Her three children were fairly compliant and responded well to their parents' leadership. All things considered, she concluded that they were a happy and healthy family.

As Allie prepared breakfast for Brandon, she reflected on all the blessings her life had brought. Brandon's career in life insurance provided well for them. They often enjoyed wonderful experiences as a family and because of home-school excursions, the outdoor zoo, the gold mine, the metal recycling plant, hiking in the nearby mountains, and vacations at the beach were all part of the family's enjoyable moments and memories.

Today, the plan was for her to sit down with Brandon over a nice breakfast, send him off to the office, feed the children, get them working on their schoolwork, and projects, give the house a light cleaning, and then head to the park for a picnic to finish the day.

There were no parts of the schedule, including cleaning, that Allie didn't enjoy. But she gained special satisfaction in watching Ava progress in her schooling. Ava was a bright six-year-old girl and really seemed to enjoy learning. She especially excelled in math and really liked reading. In fact, she had tested two grades higher in both subjects.

As Ava did her schooling, the boys would occupy themselves with the crafts that Allie provided. They were energetic and fun loving and a bit of a challenge to keep focused, but generally they obeyed and enjoyed the rewards of completing their tasks. The rewards included snacks and time outside in the play area Brandon had built.

Brandon entered the kitchen and greeted his wife with a kiss. They sat down and finished most of their breakfast together before Casey, their youngest one showed up and climbed on Brandon's lap. Casey was always the first one up and the first one to bed. Brandon enjoyed holding him as he snuggled in his dad's embrace. After a few minutes he handed the boy off to Allie and headed for the office.

The other two were up and eager to eat. Allie turned on the television and all three scrambled to the couch. They sat in their spots enjoying some cartoons as Allie got their bowls and plates ready.

After breakfast, it was schoolwork, project time, and other forms of entertainment as Allie did some laundry and straightened up the house a bit.

When lunch time came, the four of them headed for the car and the park with Allie carrying a basket containing their lunch.

At the park, she laid out a blanket instructing the children that they would eat first and then hit the playground. There were no protests and the kids jumped right into devouring their food.

After lunch the children raced to the playground. Allie chose a spot on a nearby bench and enjoyed the shade of a large elm tree. Several other children were already busy climbing, sliding, and swinging. She watched her children play and was especially proud of the way they played with the other children. Allie found herself wondering, "Why can't adults learn from the children how to get along. Why can't we love each other like these children do?" While in those thoughts she noticed something about one of the children.

It was obvious that he was afflicted with Downs Syndrome. The young boy didn't seem to be hampered by his condition and was deeply involved with everything the other children were doing. He ran, he climbed although awkwardly, and seemed to be particularly enjoying the slide.

After a couple of hours, it was time to round up the children and head to the house. With everyone secure in the car, Allie steered for home. During the ride, her curiosity got the best of her.

Looking at the children through the rear-view mirror she cautiously asked Ava, "Ava, you know that boy with the white t-shirt and blue shorts?"

"His name's Timmy" Ava replied.

"Yea, Timmy" Allie said. "Did you happen to notice anything different about him?"

"Yup" Ava replied.

"Really?" Allie asked a bit fearful of Ava's answer. "What was different about him?"

"He smiled a lot." Ava said. "He smiled all the time. I think he's a really happy boy."

Ava's answer brought a glaze of tears across Allie's eyes. And a thin smile was on her face the rest of the way home. It really was a good day!

-14-
A GOLD MEDAL HEART

"What a day! What a season!" Jim reflected as he sat aboard the team bus. It had all come together today at the high school conference track meet as his team pulled out a victory. Jim had won a gold medal in the 400 meters and set a new school record in the process.

And now, as the bus rounded the corner and headed for the gym, Jim thought about the hours of hard work and dedication that had gone into today's successful outing.

Jim looked down at his medal. It was truly beautiful. He had always dreamed of being a conference champion, of being better than the rest, of hearing his name called out over the noise of the crowd.

It really had happened he mused, as he grabbed his gear and headed for the door. Inside the locker room an announcement was made regarding the team party later that night. Everyone was excited. The entire team and a lot of the student body would be there. Jim had other plans. There was someone he had to see tonight— someone very special.

Jim drove to the hospital and thought about little Scotty. Scotty was an eight-year-old boy who lived just two doors down. Many times, when Jim would come home from practice, he'd find Scotty waiting on the front porch. He'd ask Jim if he wanted to play ball or see the frog he caught and kept securely in a jar, or even share half a cupcake. And Jim always obliged. You see, Scotty wasn't like many eight-year-old boys. He wasn't bratty or abusive. He was polite and energetic, and he was extremely curious. He never seemed to stop asking questions. And when you explained something to him, he truly listened and understood.

But now Scotty's health was declining. Six months earlier the doctors had diagnosed Scotty with leukemia, and he had steadily gone downhill. At this point the doctors gave him only days to live.

As Jim swiftly walked down the all-to-familiar hospital corridor he hoped he wasn't too late. Scotty's mom and dad were in the room and there was great concern on their faces.

"Is he awake?" Jim whispered.

"Just barely" Scotty's father choked out.

"Pastor Jordan just left" Scotty's mother added sobbing.

Jim sat on the edge of the bed and put his hand in Scotty's.

"Hey Champ! I hope you can hear me" Jim whispered trying to maintain his composure. "We sure had a great meet. I wish you could have been there. I brought you something." With his one hand still holding Scotty's, Jim drew the gold medal from his pocket and pressed it into Scotty's palm.

"This is a medal of valor" he said. "The doctors told me you deserve it."

Jim felt the tiny hand tighten around the piece.

"I gotta go now little buddy" he added. "You take care of yourself. I'll be back tomorrow."

But Jim was sure there would be no tomorrow for Scotty.

When Jim got up, Scotty's mother and father each hugged him and cried a thank you.

As Jim entered the hallway with his face wet with tears, his eye caught sight of a poster on the side of the nurse's station. It had a Bible verse which read, "Whatsoever you have done for the least of these my brethren, you have done unto me." Matthew 25:40.

"Thank you, Lord, for Scotty" was all that came to his mind as he made his way to the elevator.

-15-
LOVE NOTES

"It's so good to finally have Kevin home." Pam beamed sipping from her cup of light brown coffee and settling down at the kitchen table. It was early, but she could sleep no longer. She was so excited to have her only son home at last after almost six months of internment as an Iraqi military hostage.

While enjoying the warmth of the early morning sun, she reflected on so many things; the heartache brought on by the news of his missing; the hope both she and her husband held on to for so long; the prayers she prayed both silently and with friends; the fear and panic which tugged at her heart when she saw an official letter from the U.S. Army; and the joy and tears the two of them shed when they read how Kevin was safe and would be home soon.

Pam relived yesterday when she wondered if she'd even recognize her son at the airport. Tears clouded her eyes as she saw him emerge from the plane. He looked a good bit thinner, even gaunt, but there was no mistaking their boy. She could still feel his arms as he embraced both parents at the same time. Together they silently cried the tears of unbelief and gratitude while they stood smiling and staring at one another between hugs. And the standing ovation they received from those in the airport, will never be forgotten.

For an unknown amount of time, she bathed in the memory of the last few years and silently smiled reliving their reunion repeatedly.

"Kevin's been through so much," she thought, "We need to give him time to adjust, find a job, get settled down." Her smile faded as she pondered, "Going from a captured soldier to a citizen won't be easy. He'll need special help from lots of people."

Again, she re-entered the past and saw a small boy, eating cookies, fishing with his dad, laughing and crying almost within the same minute, and listening sweetly when she sang all the songs she could remember as she put him to bed. "He's come so far in such a short time" she breathed.

As she turned to pour more coffee, she saw a note written on a legal pad part way hidden by the phone. Pulling the pad, she read the note:

"Dear Mom,

I can't tell you how great it is to be home again! Home—the word sounds so good to me. I've dreamt of it for so long and at times, I actually felt like I was there. So much needs to be said and I hope that in time I'll find the words that I need.

It's hard to fight the memories of what I've been through. It seems unfair. For the first few weeks while being held I asked myself why? Why me? Then I stopped asking and just tried to survive.

Sometimes I was so tired and hungry and cold that I didn't know if tomorrow would come. Sometimes I didn't want it to come. I remember so many times when my body would be numb from the pain of hunger, and I would think about you and dad. And before long, almost silently I would sing a song that you had taught me when I was a kid.

Day after day, I'd see some of the other guys being dragged off their mats and off for interrogation. Or I'd hear a shot fired as the life of a young boy was taken.

Still, those sweet songs came to my mind and before long a peace would come over me. More than once I awoke calling your name and I'd swear I heard you singing.

I don't know how the others survived, but I know that those simple songs had a big part in why I'm here today.

When I was about ten years old, I remember telling you one night that I was a little too old to be sung to sleep. The look on your face was a vision I had to fight. But I was just a dumb kid then. Now I'm a man and can honestly say thanks for the songs mom! I love you!

Love, Kevin

As she folded the paper, she felt a strong hand on her shoulder and turned to face the son she'd loved before he was born. He wiped away her tears, kissed her on the forehead, and held her close as he began to hum an old familiar song.

-16-
THE PAUSE OF CARING

It was hot and sticky in the auditorium but that was okay because it was graduation, and the room was filled with excited students, families, and faculty members. Jenny Peterson, the class president, Mark Luganti, the valedictorian, and Margaret Kneed, the salutatorian, each gave short speeches which were all well organized and well received.

The class of 250 looked so healthy and attractive. There were athletes, prom queens, class officers, scholars, and the entire spectrum of personalities and physical features. They all had a look of satisfaction, eagerness, and excitement as the program ensued. Each member of the class was garbed in the school's colors and wore a small button on the front of their gowns. The button, in the school's colors of blue and white simply said, "Hang in there Matthew! We're pulling for ya!"

Matthew McDonald was a popular member of the class who was hurt seriously when a tractor-trailer ran a stop sign and struck his car broadside one night after work. Tim Marlton, also a member of the class happened by after dropping off Teresa, another classmate. He arrived just as the accident took place.

Tim stayed with Matthew through the pouring rain giving him first aid and comfort until the ambulance arrived fifteen minutes later. For two days, Matthew was in intensive care and all the medical personnel agreed that had it not been for Tim, Matthew would not have survived. The entire class was supportive of Matthew's recovery and the prognosis looked good. Still, he was missed in the congregation of graduates.

As the time came for awards and scholarships to be presented, each student sat in anticipation and curiosity regarding who the recipients would be as they were described by the various speakers.

Kelly Whittington won the Bream award for excellence in writing. Tony Preston was chosen as the school's best male athlete while Pam Jessey won the female counterpart. Mark Donovan was awarded the Burton award for community work, and Jenny Peterson was given the leadership honor. The awards and scholarships went on for over twenty-five minutes and each recipient was given appreciative applause.

At the conclusion of the program, the principal, Mrs. Kerr, rose to present the diplomas. "Before I present the diplomas," she began, "we need to recognize one more individual and present them with this plaque of gratitude. This individual was not the best student or the best athlete. He never ran for class office nor was he a member of a class committee." The class began to whisper as the principal continued. "Yet this student is an example to us all in that they displayed sacrifice and courage in giving help to a classmate in need. Please show your appreciation as I present this plaque to Tim Marlton.

Thunderous cheers began as the entire class rose to its feet while Tim worked his way to the platform. All the other awards were important and deserving of applause, but nothing short of a standing ovation would do for the person who stopped to help a friend.

-17-
A GREAT DAY!

"Hey boy! Where ya think you're goin'" the harsh voice came from the porch of an old man's house.

"I'm goin' fishin' Mr. Cleveland!" seven-year-old Jimmy Meyer replied. "I'm gonna catch me a big fish for supper tonight!"

"Oh yeah?" said Mr. Cleveland, "and where is this big fish swimmin' that you're gonna catch?"

"Down by the old school" Jimmy said enthusiastically.

"There ain't no fish in that stream boy" barked the old man. "Besides, you don't got no hook or bait. How ya spect ta catch a fish with that broom handle and string?"

Little Jimmy looked shyly at the ground and stuck his free hand in his well-worn overalls. "I dunno." He answered. "I was gonna pull 'em up when they bit the string."

"Boy, you are a fool!" the man said rising from his chair and putting his paper down. He leaned on the porch railing and continued. "Nobody in this town knows more 'bout fishin' than me and I know you ain't catchin' no fish in that stream with or without a hook-- specially not this late in the day. The place you gotta go is Wyatt Creek. And you gotta get up early in the mornin' when the fish is just gettin' up. And worms and a good hook is what you're needin.'"

Jimmy's face brightened. He leaned on his self-made fishing pole and rubbed the cowlick on his forehead which is what he did whenever he got excited. Before he remembered how mean everyone said Mr. Cleveland was, he blurted out, "Will you take me fishin' Mr. Cleveland?" And then less enthusiastically he added, "Please!"

"Boy, I got lots to do around here" Mr. Cleveland returned. "I ain't got no time to be foolin' with no kid. I ain't a babysitter 'ya know."

"Yes sir, I know, but I aint no baby either" Jimmy said in a half-defensive manner. "Maw says I'm growin' like a weed and that I'll be a man 'fore she knows it. Won't you show me how to catch a big fish Mr. Cleveland?"

The old man looked down. He gave a sigh and conceded, "Well, alright boy. I'll take you fishin'. But don't you be squawkin' this all over town. I don't want people thinkin' I'm a social worker. You be here tomorrow at sunup understand? And don't be late 'cause I ain't got no time to waste."

"Yes sir!" Jimmy blasted and he spun on his heels and raced for home.

The next morning, when Mr. Cleveland walked out on his porch, there on the steps sat Jimmy, wearing the same old shirt and over-alls he had donned the previous day.

"I see you made it" the man said slowly. "Well, let's get goin' he added, handing Jimmy a fishing pole and a can of worms. "The fish won't wait."

All the way to the creek on the other side of town, Jimmy pound-ed the old man with questions. "How come fish like worms? What the biggest star in the universe? How far is China?" These and more came at Mr. Cleveland at a regular pace.

Just before they reached the woods, the elderly fellow finally commented, "You sure do ask a lot of questions boy!"

"Yup," responded Jimmy. "Mom says I'm quizitive natured." The old man just raised his eyebrows at the response.

When they reached the stream, Mr. Cleveland gave a short dis-course on trout fishing and then set Jimmy up on a log where the stream made a turn while he moved a little further upstream.

After about two minutes, Jimmy shouted, "You got anything yet?"

"No" said Mr. Cleveland. "But ya gotta be real quiet."

"Me neither" shot Jimmy. "I hope I catch somethin' soon."

"Boy" Mr. Cleveland shouted in a whisper, "You're gonna scare every fish from here to Kentucky."

"Sorry," said Jimmy, pausing for a moment before asking, "Do fish have ears?"

"No, not like you and me son," Mr. Cleveland replied half smiling and looking hopelessly at Jimmy who was looking under rocks for salamanders.

The morning continued like this and by ten o'clock Jimmy had skipped sixteen stones, caught two frogs, a crawfish, went swimming, watched three squirrels play, threw a mud clog at some birds, climbed a tree, and found four salamanders, but to no one's surprise, neither he, nor Mr. Cleaveland had caught any fish.

Normally, coming home empty-handed would have bothered Mr. Cleveland. But midway through the outing he had put his pole down and talked to Jimmy while watching him in newfound wonder as Jimmy moved about with boyish curiosity.

In front of Mr. Cleveland's house, Jimmy looked up and grinned at his friend. "Thanks for takin' me fishin' Mr. Cleveland" he said.

"Sure thing!" replied the old man as he reached down and mussed up Jimmy's hair.

With that, Jimmy headed for home leaving Mr. Cleveland watching him glide along stopping only long enough to pick up a long weeping willow branch and use it to sting the backs of some make believe horses.

A small smile creased the old man's face. He turned toward his house and nodded slightly. It had been a good day!

-18-
REUNITED

Nothing had gone the way it was supposed to. All the dreams and opportunities had faded and dried up for Laura. At one time she had everything a teen-age girl could want: a lovely home, nice clothes, spending money, and most importantly, a loving and caring family.

Why she turned her back on all that she didn't know. As she stood under a canopy sheltering her from the pouring rain, she fought to keep the tears from flowing. Her mind reflected on all the special times she had with her family. Thoughts of love and protection flooded her mind.

She also thought of that night, nearly two years ago, when she and her father had gotten into a heated argument over her going out with a boy he didn't approve of. She soon found out he was right. She was sixteen and Jerry was twenty and the night she ran away, she found herself in Jerry's apartment. Things were fine at first, but then the money she had saved ran out and after Jerry had gotten enough of what he wanted, he threw her out.

Her pride kept her from going home. She moved to the city where she thought it would be easier to find work, but all her avenues turned into dead end alleys, and she was forced to do things she'd always looked down on.

And now, almost two years later she'd experienced enough for three lifetimes. She'd made money by selling herself and had tried nearly every drug on the street. She'd been beaten, robbed and infected and had nowhere to turn except to the kind of people who only mean trouble. So finally, after all the time and all her tries she found herself on a street covered with filth and danger.

Several times in the last few months she'd tried to call home but each time she hung up as the phone was answered. But tonight, she was determined to make contact with her family again.

With a lump in her throat, she pressed the *Go* button as she had tried to do so many times before. Each breath came with difficulty as she waited for an answer. So many times, she longed to speak with the person who answered the phone. It was her dad.

"Hello."

That single word brought tears to Laura's eyes. She had rehearsed a complete dialogue, but her thoughts melted and all that escaped her throat was,

"Daddy."

Instantly came the response.

"Laura!"

"Daddy, I want to come home." She strained with her tears freely flowing.

"Where are you?"

"I'm in Manhattan. On the corner of 44th and Broadway in a diner."

"Honey, stay there. I'll be there in about an hour. I miss you and I love you" he choked.

"I love you too daddy!" she whispered.

She clicked off the phone with those last seven words still screaming through her mind. "I miss you and I love you." For the next hour that's all she could hear or think about.

Time stood still. Inside a diner, Laura sipped four cups of coffee with her eyes fixed on the street looking for the familiar frame of her father.

Finally. Finally, he stood in the doorway. Her Dad! Simultaneously, and without a word, they rushed toward each other, ignoring the stares of the customers. They embraced briefly as both began to cry and then her father spoke,

"Laura! Laura! It's so good to see you. Are you okay?"

She nodded, "I'm fine Daddy. I just want to come home."

"Sure Kitten, let's go."

And they walked to the car arm in arm in silence. Few words

were spoken for the next hour. They just drove through the rain both with grateful hearts.

-19-
RETURNED KINDNESS

Kathy loved the woods. And on summer days like this she could spend a lifetime in a few minutes drinking in all God had created. It had been a very busy Saturday morning and she had spent much time cleaning, washing, and straightening up their little home on the edge of town.

And now she had some time to relax a bit and enjoy the beauty of her surroundings in total isolation from family, friends, and the cares of her world.

It was cool and pleasant deep in the woods as she sat on the edge of a log in the area that had grown to be her favorite spot. She sat next to a small stream and watched the activity that sprang from it. She loved watching a frog swim or a turtle poke his head up as he waited for the area to settle. Even the insects were some-what entertaining as they busied themselves in total oblivion to her presence. The air smelled musty but in a sweet sort of way and a gentle breeze caressed her skin as she listened to the music of the ever-flowing brook.

The entire area seemed to be like God's way of orchestrating peace in a topsy-turvy world. One could sit for hours and drink deeply of the beauty and serenity of this unspoiled Eden-like place.

After thirty minutes of enjoying her solace Kathy knew that she must be returning home. Not that her husband Jeff would worry about her—he knew where she was. In fact, he'd been there several times himself. It's just that Kathy had some things she needed to get done before dinner. With these thoughts in mind, she forced herself from her perch and sighing deeply leaned toward home.

As she took her first step, out of the corner of her eye, she noticed something moving and heard a rustling sound. Turning quickly, she saw leaves being scattered at the base of an old tree. She moved closer until she could interpret the disturbance.

On the other side of the tree, she saw a small squirrel with his hind leg caught in a metal trap. Quickly she moved and bent down to free the struggling animal. But each time she moved close to him, he scratched the back of her outstretched hand and tried to bite her.

Kathy backed away for a moment and then found a large branch. With the branch she was able to apply enough pressure on the spring so the squirrel could slip his leg out. His leg didn't seem to be badly damaged. Once free, the squirrel hopped over to a small bush, then turned and looked directly at Kathy before scampering away. Kathy watched him disappear and then turned to walk home happily.

When she shared with her husband what had transpired during her retreat in the woods, he commented amusingly that one of the basic characteristics that separated man from the animal world is the ability to outwardly communicate gratitude.

Kathy was to learn differently. For the next day, when she opened the back door of their home, she found a small green acorn on the sill. She smiled, picked it up and sighed, "Maybe we're not so different after all."

-20-
THE MOST SPECIAL DAY

Jim and Teresa were especially excited that Saturday morning. Today was the day that Marissa, their eight-year-old daughter would be competing in the Special Olympics for the first time. Marissa struggled with a severe case of Autism and looking after her consumed so much of their time. Still, they carried a love for her that rivaled any parent's love for their little one.

The day Marissa was born everything seemed to be normal. She smiled, cried, slept, and fussed just like any baby. But shortly after bringing her home, they began to notice some behavior in her that puzzled them. Though she ate and slept well, she seemed to go into a stare at times and Jim and Teresa struggled to get her attention. They considered whether she was deaf, but her hearing checked out as normal. They thought that perhaps she was experiencing Petit mal seizures, but the doctors ruled that out as well. It wasn't until she was about three-years old that the doctors concluded that she was Autistic.

With this knowledge they began to plan various ways to care for her and to meet her needs. Marissa was a gentle child. She seemed to enjoy being with her family and got quite agitated when one or both of her parents wasn't around.

Marissa had a particular look she gave when there was something she enjoyed. She would put her head to the side, smile, and give a high-pitched squeal to show that she was happy. Likewise, when she was frightened or in need of something, she would put her head down and rock gently back and forth.

Jim and Teresa did everything they could to make sure that Marissa was healthy and well cared for. Her room was filled with stuffed animals, colored drawings, and music. A warm bath with plenty of bubbles were part of Marissa's routine and she got excited each evening as *bath time* approached.

Jim wasn't sure why, but he entered Marissa in the 50-yard dash. She enjoyed running at home and spent a good deal of her play time chasing dad. Teresa brought Marissa over to the local high school track to get her familiar with the surroundings and to run her race a few times. That Saturday morning, they arrived at the meet and Jim checked Marissa in.

After a few events Jim walked Marissa over to the starting line. She was in the lane closest to the stands which made it easier for her to hear her parents shouting words of encouragement.

When the whistle blew Marissa seemed to know exactly what to do. She took off like an experienced runner and to the great surprise of her parents, she won! Jim and Teresa were overjoyed. They couldn't have been happier if Marissa had won the state championship. But their excitement climbed to an even higher level when she raised her hands and yelled, "I won! I won!"

Simultaneously, Jim and Teresa burst into tears. They hugged each other and held their embraces. Over and over, they yelled, "Way to go Marissa! That-a -girl! Good job!" Jim and Teresa escorted Marissa over to the awards stand and a blue ribbon was pinned to her shirt. They never stopped crying.

An official noticed their continual tears and asked them if everything was alright. "No! Nothing's wrong" Jim said. "In fact, everything's great. We just heard our daughter speak for the first time."

-21-
A YOUNG FAN'S EYES

It was a tough night on the gridiron for Wayne and his high school teammates. Though they played hard, they were outmanned and outgunned by the Rams, and they lost by two touchdowns. Wayne couldn't understand what had gone wrong. He thought they were prepared, and he knew they were in good condition, but it seemed like everything they did just wasn't enough.

As captain, he tried to motivate the team to keep fighting, but the spark just wasn't there. Every play they tried to run on offense the Rams' defense had an answer for. And the best they could do on defense was to slow them down a bit. Wayne even committed two penalties himself, one of which gave the Rams a first down.

After a wrap up talk from Coach McKenney, Wayne showered and got dressed. He was one of the last players to leave the locker room and had already decided not to join the others at *The Burger Palace*. He got his bag and started the long walk home.

Wayne loved football and he loved winning. They had a good team and with one game to go, they had only lost two. But tonight, felt especially hard for him. He felt they should have won. He knew they were better than their opponent and certainly better than they showed. They just couldn't get it together when it really counted. He tried to shake the game off his mind, but it kept coming back and driving his spirits to the bottom of his shoes. Home was only a half-mile away, but he felt like he was walking to the edge of the world.

When he got home his mother greeted him with a hug and his dad gave him a firm pat on the back and a few words of encouragement. Over a small snack of burger bites, French fries, and a large glass of milk, his mom explained how his cousin Casey had gone to the game with them and was spending the night in the guest room.

Casey was six years old, and idolized Wayne. Wherever Wayne went Casey wanted to be by his side, asking questions and telling stories. Wayne knew that Casey was at the game because every time he came off the field, he heard the unmistakable high-pitched voice of his cousin calling out to him.

Wayne sat down on the edge of his bed. He pulled the covers off his pillow and found a note on a plain piece of paper. The note was from his young cousin and brought a small smile to his face.

I saw your game tonight. You did good! Your a good ~~football~~ football player! From Casey

With the note was a single stick of gum. He took the gum, put it inside the note, folded the paper around it and tossed it on his dresser.

Wayne leaned back on his pillow, slid his feet under the covers, and closed his exhausted eyes. He smiled again and thought, "At least someone thinks I played a good game." And with that thought, he drifted off to a deep sleep knowing that tomorrow would bring a new day.

-22-
A FOREVER GIFT

Rob was a was fifteen-year-old who lived with his mother and father on their struggling farm in Buffalo, New York. He knew his dad loved him but had not understood it until a few days before Christmas. He overheard what his father was saying to his mother.

"Mary, I hate to call Rob in the mornings. He's growing so fast, and he needs his sleep. If you could see how he sleeps when I go in to wake him up! I wish I could manage alone."

"Well, you can't Adam." His wife's voice was brisk. "Besides, he isn't a child anymore. It's time he took his turn."

"Yes," his father said slowly. "But I sure do hate to wake him."

When he heard those words, something in him was aroused: his father loved him! He had never thought of it before, taking for granted the tie of their blood. Neither his father nor his mother had much time to talk about love. There was always so much to do on the farm.

Now that he knew his father loved him, there would be no more loitering in the mornings and having to be called repeatedly. He got up after that, stumbling with sleep, and pulled on his clothes, his eyes half shut.

And then on the night before Christmas, he lay for a few minutes thinking about the next day. They were poor, and most of the excitement was in the turkey they had raised themselves, and in the mince pies his mother made. His mother and father always bought something he needed, usually something like a warm jacket, but often something more, such as a book. And he saved and bought them each something, too.

He wished he had a better present for his father. As usual, he had gone to the ten-cent store and bought a small trinket. It had seemed nice enough until he lay thinking the night before Christmas, and then he wished he had heard his father and mother talking in time for him to save for something better.

He lay on his side, his head supported by his elbow, and looked out of his window. The stars were bright, much brighter than he ever remembered them being, and he could see almost every detail on the side of the house.

Then a thought came to him as clear as the moon-lit yard. Why should he not give his father a special gift, too, out there in the barn? He could get up early, earlier than 4 o'clock, and he could creep into the barn and get all the milking done. He'd do it alone, milk and clean up, and then when his father went in to start the milking, he'd see it all done. And he would know who had done it.

At quarter to three, he got up and put on his clothes. He crept downstairs, careful of the creaky boards, and let himself out. The big star hung lower over the barn roof, a reddish gold. The cows looked at him, sleepy and surprised.

He whispered a good morning and fetched some hay for each cow before getting the milking pail and the big milk cans.

He had never milked all alone before, but it seemed almost easy. He kept thinking about his father's surprise. His father would come in and call him, saying that he would get things started while Rob was getting dressed. He'd go to the barn, open the door, and then he'd go to get the two big empty milk cans.

But they wouldn't be waiting or empty; they'd be standing in the milk house, filled.

The task went smoothly and didn't carry the weight of a chore. It was something else, a gift to his father who loved him. He finished, the two milk cans were full, and he covered them and closed the milk house door carefully, making sure of the latch. He put the stool in its place by the door and hung up the clean milk pail. Then he went out of the barn and barred the door behind him.

Back in his room, he had only a minute to pull off his clothes in the darkness and jump into bed, for he heard his father moving about. He put the covers over his head to silence his quick breathing. The door opened.

"Rob!" his father called. "We have to get up, son, even if it is Christmas."

"Aw-right," he said sleepily.

"I'll go on out," his father said. "I'll get things started."

The door closed and he lay still, laughing to himself. In just a few minutes his father would know. His dancing heart was ready to jump from his body.

The minutes were endless- ten, fifteen, he did not know how many. Then he heard his father's steps again. The door opened and he lay still holding onto the pretense of sleep.

"Rob!"

"Yes, Dad?"

His father was laughing, a queer sobbing sort of laugh. "Thought you'd fool me, didn't you?" His father was standing beside him, pulling away the cover.

"It's for Christmas, Dad!"

He found his father and clutched him in a great hug. He felt his father's arms go around him. It was dark, and they could not see each other's face, but they sensed each other's heart.

"Son, thank you. Nobody ever did a nicer thing."

"Oh, Dad, I want you to know, I do want to do good!" The words broke from him of their own will and couldn't find their way out. His heart was bursting with Joy.

"Well, I reckon I can go back to bed and sleep," his father said after a moment.

A couple of hours later, Rob got up, pulled on his clothes again, and worked his way downstairs. Soon the sun was creeping up where the stars had been. Oh, what a Christmas! And how his heart had nearly burst again with shyness and pride as his father told his mother about how he, Rob, had gotten up all by himself and had completed all the morning work.

Turning to Rob he said, "The best Christmas gift I ever had, and I'll remember it, son, every year on Christmas morning, so long as I live."

And true to his word, his dad always remembered it mentioning it every year as Christmas day approached. He labeled it the best gift anyone had ever given him, and Rob called it the best gift he'd ever given. But both saw it as it truly was, a gift of sincere love.

(Adapted from Pearl S. Buck-Christmas Day in the Morning.)

-23-

THE PEACE OF FRIENDSHIP

The squadron had been immersed in a short dog fight with six Japanese fighters. Their group had shot down two of the enemies' planes and had lost one of their own. In one of the strafings, the pilot had been slightly wounded and one of the other crew members had been killed as enemy bullets poured through the thin metal canvas. Still, they continued to fight.

Robert had manned the rear gun and never saw the Japanese plane attack from the front. Then as their plane swooped low over the water and began to climb the pilot yelled the words no soldier wants to hear, "We're hit! We're hit!" His words rang out above the noise of the fighter jet and each man knew this was more than a piercing of the shell. "Prepare for impact!" The four men aboard the *Tomahawk* showed no delay as they braced for a collision with the Pacific Ocean. The pilot did his best to control the plane, but it spun 360 degrees before it hit the water.

As the plane violently turned, the force kept Robert from reaching the safety straps and he was hurled from the craft.

The force of the fall drove the air from his lungs and Robert struggled to breathe. Out of the corner of his eye he saw the plane hit the water and burst into flames. He knew there could be no survivors.

Regaining his breath, Robert did a mental evaluation of his body. He felt a little pain in his back and his head was throbbing. Looking down he saw that his left arm had a deep cut just above the elbow. Beyond that, he seemed to be unharmed. While treading water, he realized that his floatation vest was holding him. This gave him time to figure out what to do.

Very soon darkness would be settling in and he knew he couldn't last long in these waters. Either the cold would do him in or the enemy patrol boats would find him. His heavy fatigues and vest helped him maintain a minimal amount of heat, but he knew he had to be active in order to generate more heat.

He had no idea where he was, so he began to slowly swim. In just a few minutes the sky became completely black. This compounded his confusion. He had been swimming for over an hour but for all he knew, he may have made a complete circle. As the cold and fatigue raced for control, he joined the battle to remain conscious. His fight for consciousness was lost to fatigue and Robert drifted with the sea.

Before daybreak, Robert opened one eye but only saw a blur in the darkness. Then in great surprise he realized that his feet were behind him, and he could feel something on his chest. The sound and splashing of the waves clued him in to the fact that he was on a beach. Robert fought to bring himself upright but only managed to roll over and sit up. With his elbows holding his knees, he breathed a prayer of thankfulness for his survival against the unforgiving ocean.

But where was he? And where was the enemy? He knew he was in the Pacific corridor but had no idea where. After a good while sitting and trying to gain control of his mental faculties, Robert rolled to his knees and with great effort was able to stand. His ability to walk slowly returned and he gingerly stumbled away from the waves.

A steady stream of blood was coming from his wounded arm and on further examination he found that he had suffered a deep gash in his triceps. This was now accompanied by a severe amount of pain. With a great deal of struggle and the edge of a sharp rock, he was able to cut off part of his sleeve and repurpose it for a bandage.

Daylight came along and to the best that he could discern, he was on a small island. He found a couple of coconuts and after using a rock as a tool was soon partaking of the juices as well as the meat. As his strength began to return, he decided to quietly explore the island. Eventually he climbed to the top of a ridge and could see that he in fact was on a small island with no other islands or signs of life in sight.

Robert's survival training went into effect. He knew what his priorities were: heat, clean water, food, and shelter. He found clean water by way of a small waterfall and shelter was provided by a large overhanging rock. He already knew the island carried coconuts and was sure he could manage to catch some fish.

Creating heat however was a problem. He knew he could start a fire, but also knew that a fire increased his chances of being captured. Still, he understood that the returning night would be cold and decided to take a chance. He would wait until nightfall so the smoke would not be seen. To prevent anyone from seeing the flames, he would shield the fire on the edge of the rock.

The wound on his arm was still very painful and continued to bleed when he moved it the wrong way. The salt water had helped control the bleeding, but it had increased his pain greatly. He did his best to use his other arm but often needed the use of both limbs. Without proper medicine, he knew that infection would eventually set in.

Canvasing the beach, Robert found several clams and two crabs. Dinner would be served at the onset of darkness. His next chore was to build a fire primarily using one arm. He put the end of a small twig on a rock and surrounded it with dry grass. Then he used his boot lace and another stick to make a bow-like structure that he wrapped around the upright twig. A rock held the top of the twig, and his bad arm held the rock. In this way he was able to rotate the twig back and forth and generate heat and light the grass. Before long he had a blazing fire and was enjoying both its warmth and the meal he cooked by it.

Then out of the darkness he saw a man standing on the edge of the firelight. Robert was startled and let out an abrupt though muffled shout and immediately put his good arm up for protection. The stranger stepped closer, and Robert was relieved to see that he was unarmed. He could tell that he was Japanese but also knew that he was not military. The man bowed in a greeting, stepped closer and patted his own arm signifying that he noticed the wound on Robert's arm. Robert's defenses dropped. He pushed a stick with crab meat on it in the man's direction and the man bowed again, pulled it off, and popped it in his mouth.

He patted his chest and said the word "Mamori Tai."

Robert repeated the move and said, "Robert." He bowed again, pointed at Robert's arm, and signaled for him to follow. Robert rose and with only the moon lighting the trail, followed the man.

A few minutes later Robert found himself standing in front of Mamori Tai's home. It was very obvious that the man had lived there for quite a while. His house was well built and showed signs of withstanding both winds and storms. Inside, it was complete with everything a man needed to live alone on an island. It had a shelf holding a single book, a storage area, and a bed made of vines and suspended from the floor. Mamori Tai signaled for Robert to sit down. Robert complied and Momori Tai disappeared inside his hut and emerged moments later with a wooden box. He gingerly removed the blood-soaked bandage from Robert's arm and tossed it aside. Then he gently applied some ointment and wrapped it with a small piece of cloth. A slight burning sensation was felt but it only served to reassure Robert that the solution was working. Very soon his arm was securely bandaged, and Robert gave a "Thank you" smile.

Both men sat by the small fire outside of Mamori Tai's hut. They tried to communicate but the language barrier proved to be too much for them. When the night grew long, Mamori Tai signaled Robert to lay down handing him a small blanket. Robert lay by the fire and soon fell into an exhausted sleep.

The language difficulties never disappeared completely but the men never let it get in the way of their cooperative relationship. Month after month, they fished together, gathered water and firewood, and communicated using broken bits from each other's language and plenty of hand motions. Robert learned that Mamori Tai had landed on the island when a storm took his fishing boat down. He lost his friend to the sea and had been on the island for over a year.

Then one day and quite unexpectedly a fishing boat was seen off the east side of the island. The men built a large signal fire and in short order were shaking hands with the fishermen. One of the men who spoke English fairly well informed them that the war had ended six weeks ago, with the Japanese surrendering to the U.S. They agreed to take the men aboard, and within a week both men were united with their families and moving ahead with their separate lives.

The men stayed in touch with one another even visiting each other a couple of times. The war had ended for the two countries with a signed agreement, but it ended for Mamori Tai and Robert with a caring and helpful hand that forged a life-long friendship.

-24-
AGELESS HEARTS

If ever a friendship started by accident, it was the one between Jeffrey and Mr. Biser. Jeffery was a ten-year-old boy who lived with his family on Elk Street in the suburbs of Philadelphia. He was an active boy and quite typical in his energy and love of adventure. He held an average affinity for school with average grades but possessed an imagination that excelled beyond his peers.

Mr. Biser was an elderly man of eighty-one years who lived on Beacon Street around the corner from Jeffrey. For his age, he was fairly healthy, although he struggled with a good bit of arthritis in his left knee. This gave him a pronounced limp and limited his mobility. Having lost his wife to cancer ten years earlier, he lived alone and kept mainly to himself. He had no other family members and had settled into a lifestyle of independence and aloneness.

Early one Saturday morning, Jeffery was blazing a trail on his bike to meet up with some friends to play baseball at the park. He navigated the turn onto Beacon Street and was picking up speed. When he steered his bike onto the sidewalk, he hit the edge of the curb with his back tire flattening it and tossing him sideways on the sidewalk. He didn't hit hard but immediately noticed a small tear in his jeans and a scrape on his knee.

As he sat on the lawn examining the damage both to his bike and his knee, he heard a voice from the porch behind him.

"You okay son?"

Jeffrey turned and saw Mr. Biser sitting on his front porch with the morning paper in hand.

"Yeah, I'm fine" Jeffery returned. "I got a flat and a scrape."

"Let's have a look" Mr. Biser said as he dropped his paper, stood up and grabbed his cane heading for the steps.

Jeffery gathered himself and began walking toward the house. He started with a limp which disappeared after a few steps.

Mr. Biser negotiated down the two steps easily and looked down at Jeffrey who took a seat on the bottom step.

"Not too bad" he said. "I've seen worse, and I've had worse. Let me get you a band aid." With that he turned and disappeared into the house.

Moments later he returned with an unwrapped band aid. He handed it to Jeffery who peeled and applied it in one smooth move.

"Thanks" he said looking up at Mr. Biser.

"You're welcome." The man returned.

"What's your name young man?"

"Jeffrey" he said, "What's yours?"

"Gary Biser" he said extending his hand.

Jeffrey rose to his feet and took the old man's hand at the same time.

"Well, I gotta get going. Gotta take my bike back."

"Be careful" Mr. Biser said.

With that, Jeffrey bent down and retrieved his glove, slid it over the handlebar and pushed his bike toward home.

Two days later while riding his repaired bike, Jeffrey turned the corner to see Mr. Biser standing by the curb looking down. He stopped immediately and dismounted.

"Hey Mr. Biser! Whatcha doin'?"

"Starin' at my keys. It's what people do when they step into the stupid zone"

Standing next to Mr. Biser and looking down, Jeffrey realized what happened.

"I just came home and stepped out to get the mail. But when I opened the mailbox, I dropped my keys, and there they are in the storm drain. Maybe I can hook them with a coat hanger."

"I think I can reach 'em" Jeffrey said as he lay on his belly and squeezed his arm through the opening in the iron grate.

A few seconds later he handed the lost keys to Mr. Biser and so began a friendship between a man of great experience and a boy of endless energy.

Jeffery began spending more and more time at Mr. Biser's. Sitting on the porch, drinking lemonade or iced tea, while listening to the experiences the elderly man's long life had given him. Mr. Biser's stories were amazing, and his ability to share them had the young boy captivated. Scuba diving, fighting in Korea, working through the depression, sky diving, flying a plane, and working as a police officer in New York City, were just a few of the categories from which endless stories seemed to pour from the old man's memory stores. And Jeffrey seemed to have his ears glued to every word that came from the ancient tongue.

Occasionally Jeffrey's friends would pressure him into joining them in some adventure sometimes even ridiculing him for spending so much time with his elderly friend. But Jeffrey worked his way past the comments and so often found himself sitting with the old man asking questions, gaining wisdom, and being entertained by a story.

As Jeffrey advanced through Middle School and High School, he and Mr. Biser grew to be great friends. Sometimes the old man would give him a chore to do and reward him with a few dollars. It wasn't that he couldn't do it himself, but it was more of an opportunity to bless his young friend by sliding a little cash his way.

Both Jeffrey's Grandfathers had passed away, so in many ways, Mr. Biser became his surrogate grandfather. So it was not a surprise when Mr. Biser attended both Jeffrey's high school and college graduation ceremonies, nor was it a surprise for Jeffrey to be asked to speak at the funeral of his dear friend.

But the storied friendship didn't end with the passing of Mr. Biser. Jeffrey became a writer. Along with writing for various magazines, he became a writer of books. Many of the stories and articles he wrote had their seeds planted in the soil of Mr. Biser's life. Jeffrey expressed himself in both fiction and non-fiction venues and wound up with several books on the *Best Sellers* list. He even had one of his books adopted into several school's sixth grade curriculum. It was an instructional book on making wise choices. Packed with wisdom and housed as a novel, the book was titled, "Mr Biser, Life's Adviser."

So the friendship that started with a scraped knee and a dropped set of keys lives on in the mind of Jeffrey and on bookshelves all across the country. And the world is a better place because of the friendship that grew between an aging man and a growing boy.

-25-

A SWEET SOUL

Pam pulled into the restaurant parking lot and helped her two children out.

They had behaved well in the store and were told that they could order anything they wanted. Six-year-old Josh and four-year-old Caleb instantly yelled out "Hot dogs!" Pam knew without asking that there had to be some French fries with plenty of ketchup to go with their order.

Making their way inside, they were shown to a table near the window in the middle of the restaurant. Pam knew that a window seat would provide plenty of entertainment for the boys and her conclusion was realized almost immediately.

Josh looked at a sportscar and shared his thoughts about how fast it went and how the man was probably going to the racetrack. Caleb chimed in about how he was going to have a big fast car when he grew up. On the sidewalk a dog walked by and both boys saw it at the same time. "That's a friendly dog" Josh said. "I'll bet he likes hot dogs" Caleb offered and both boys chuckled. The boys loudly shared their findings while a smile graced mom's face the entire time.

Soon the waitress came over to take their orders. Before she could ask, the boys spoke up and placed their order. "Hot dogs and a coke!" they said together. "And French fries with lots of ketchup" Josh added. The waitress smiled at the boys and took Pam's order. She returned shortly with their drinks and the boys were satisfied but still excited.

When the meal arrived, Josh asked if he could say grace. The family bowed their heads and the six-year-old said, "God is good. God is great. Thank you for the food, and I would even thank you more if mom gets us ice cream for dessert. And Liberty and justice for all! Amen."

Those within earshot laughed out loud. But one customer leaned into her friend and said, "That's what's wrong with this country. Kids today don't even know how to pray. Asking God for ice-cream! That's ridiculous!"

When the words reached Josh's ears he leaned into his mother's side and burst into tears. "Did I pray the wrong way, Mom? Is God mad at me?" Pam pulled him onto her lap and gave him a reassuring squeeze. "No darling! You did a great job and I happen to know that your prayer brought a smile to the face of God and all His angels."

Just then, an elderly gentleman approached the table. He winked at Josh and said, "I happen to know that God thought that was a great prayer." Sitting up and wiping away a tear Josh said, "Really?" "Cross my heart." Then the man leaned forward, nodded his head toward the table where the woman was seated and said, "Too bad she never asks God for ice cream. A little ice cream is good for the soul."

Pam smiled and thanked the man for his comments. A few minutes later, the boys had finished their meals and were wiggling in their seats as the waitress brought them each a dish of their favorite ice cream. Without hesitation, Caleb had jumped into his, but Josh sat looking at the treat before him.

Without a word, he picked up his dish, walked it over to the table where the lady sat and placed it in front of her. Then he smiled with a smile as big as his heart and said, "This is for you. Ice cream is good for the soul, and my soul is good already."

Smiles were seen all around the restaurant and Pam fought to control her tears. When the three of them got up to leave they were informed at the register that their bill had been paid. When Josh asked about it, Pam simply said, "That is what we call the smile of God."

(Adapted from "Ice Cream is Good for the Soul" Author unknown)

-26-

THE GRAND SLAM OF FRIENDSHIP

Mitch's heart was alive with excitement. Everything was going as he had dreamed. Just three more batters and the game would be over. His team, the Cougars, would be undefeated and head into the high school regional play-offs seeded first.

They had played well all year and had met all the expectations of both the coach as well as the fans. Today, as predicted, they were beating the Indians 6-0. But this game meant even more to Mitch because as he had hoped, he would pitch his fourth shut-out breaking the old school record. The newspapers had written about it and the fans anticipated it and finally in the top of the seventh inning, it was happening. But it was even better than that. Mitch was in the midst of pitching his first perfect game with no hits, no walks, and no errors.

Mitch felt strong as he hurled the ball on-line to his catcher. He had an array of pitches in his arsenal, and all seemed to be effective today. After three pitches the first batter popped out to the catcher.

"One down, two to go!" Mitch muttered facing away from the plate and rubbing the ball.

Mitch had not faced the second batter before but knew what was happening. The opposing coach had measured his chances and decided to let some of the substitutes bat during this, their final game of the season.

His first pitch was a fast ball right down the center of the plate and passed the batter for a called strike. The second was an outside curve just missing the corner to even up the count. Two pitches later the second batter was walking slowly back to the dugout pounding the end of the bat.

"One more time! Just one more time" he said over and over waiting for the next and hopefully last batter. After a short delay, a challenger emerged from the Indians' shelter. Mitch turned to watch him approach the plate. He couldn't believe his eyes. It was Sean Livingston!

He and Sean had grown up next to each other and grew to be great friends. Sean was different. Although he was fun to be with, Mitch learned as they grew that Sean had a learning disability and would no longer be in his class. In fact, Sean began to go to a special school after 2nd grade. But the boys continued to spend time together and Mitch always looked out for Sean when other boys picked on him.

At age fifteen, Sean's family moved to another town and their close relationship was wrinkled. He often talked with Sean on the phone and occasionally ran across him at the mall but they each had developed new friends and relied less on each other's company. Sean had called Mitch before the season began and told him how he had made the team, but Mitch knew that he was more of a manager or a mascot than a player.

Before the game started, Mitch and Sean shared some time together. Sean congratulated him on a great year and the two talked over some of the things they had done while growing up with one another. They wished each other luck and headed for their respective sides.

And now they met again in a totally unpredicted arena. They were pitted against each other as pitcher and batter. Mitch's mind tossed him back and forth emotionally. Sean stepped to the plate in a uniform a size too large and banged the club on the plate as he had seen all the players do.

"Well, here goes nothin'" breathed Mitch.

He hurled the ball right down the middle of the plate as Sean watched it go by-a solid strike! The next pitch sailed across the sweet spot again and Sean missed it swinging too late.

Mitch held the ball in his glove, looked at Sean and turned his hand over, tipping his head to one side as if to say, "Come on, will ya?" Sean recognized the sign from their days of growing up together. This is what Mitch did when he was frustrated with Sean.

Everyone in the stadium knew the game was over and would end in a strike-out. Mitch would get his shut-out breaking the school record and pitching a perfect game while doing it. The Cougars would head to the playoffs undefeated, and the Indians would meander home after a lackluster season.

The count was 0-2. Mitch quickly wound up and lobbed the ball to the catcher. Sean, again swinging late, made contact and the ball curved lazily above the outstretched glove of the first baseman coming to a stop between the infield and the outfield. No play was made and moments later Sean stood tall and proud on first base.

When the ball came back to the mound, Mitch rubbed it hard, called time out and trotted to first. Sean met him smiling and clapping his hands. Mitch handed him the ball, patted him on the shoulder and said, "Good job buddy" and headed back to the hill.

Three pitches later, the game was over. The Cougars went into the play-offs undefeated, the Indians rolled home, Sean had gotten the only hit of his young life, and Mitch had rekindled a friendship that lasted all their days.

-27-
THE RING OF LOVE

No words were spoken. It was just a simple movement of the hand. To an outsider, the gesture may have been quite confusing. But for Peggy, Jerry, and the rest of the family, it brought smiles and tears to the eyes.

Jerry's health was in rapid decline, and the family members were all gathered around his bed. He had been struggling with heart and lung issues for quite some time but now was hanging on to the edge of life. The family had been called in and had not left his side for three consecutive days. They had no need of the medical staff to inform them that the end was near.

Jerry and Peggy had been married for almost 60 years. They worked hard on the family's North Carolina farm and had the pleasure of raising three children to adulthood. They were blessed with a solid work ethic as well as an endearing sense of humor. Their love and care for each other was easily noted by all who came to know them.

Jerry was the consummate protector and provider, and Peggy was endowed with a heart that cared deeply for others and held the family together. Theirs was a love that brought them through the difficulties of the Korean war, economic downturns, droughts, floods, health issues, and a host of physical challenges.

And through it all they stayed together counterpunching the difficulties life sent their way. They learned to bear down when the work was hard, kneel down when things got tough, and laugh whenever they had the chance. It was by no means an easy life, but by all means a good life.

Jerry began a tradition on their first anniversary and kept it up throughout their marriage. Sometime during the celebration of their anniversary, he would extend his hand to Peggy and slip her wedding ring off her finger. He'd take the ring, hold it over his heart, and without a word, slide it back on her hand. This had gone on for almost 60 years and they were the only times the ring had ever left her hand.

And now with the entire family around his bedside, they watched Jerry in such a weakened state, gently tap his left ring finger with his right hand. He wasn't speaking but he was repeatedly mouthing the words, "One more time. One more time, one more time..."

Immediately Peggy knew what to do. She slowly pulled her wedding ring off. Then she gently turned Jerry's hand over and put the ring in his palm. She moved his thumb and index finger together and slid the ring between them. While holding his fingers with her right hand, she slid her ring finger through the opening. Jerry nodded slightly and gave a small smile.

Then the beloved man breathed deeply, held his breath for a few short moments, exhaled and left this earth. The tears from those standing by flowed easily and abundantly. And to this day, the memories and love they built and nurtured live on in Peggy's heart.

-28-
A DEEPER LOVE

Five-year-old Caleb sat at the dinner table across from his mom and dad Walt and Heather. Having finished dinner, his father looked at him and said, "Caleb, your mom and I have something to tell you that's very important." The young boy gave them all his attention without saying a word.

"Your little sister Sarah is very sick. In fact, she's sick with the same disease that you had when you were born. The doctors say that if she doesn't get the same type of help you got, she won't be able to live.

Sarah was born two weeks earlier and had not been able to leave the hospital. She had a rare blood disorder that required her to be under medical observation and treatment. The prognosis was that she would remain stable for some time but that the disease would increase with her growth, and she would be unable to sustain life.

Caleb's lips quivered a bit and he nodded. Normally, he was a fairly quiet boy and his parents weren't sure how he would receive the news.

His mother chimed in, "Caleb, the doctors want to check you to see if you have what she needs that you can give to her. They want to run some tests to check you out. So tomorrow we're going to take you to the hospital to give them a little sample of your blood."

Caleb's dad added, "It's going to hurt but just a tiny bit and it won't take long. While we're at the hospital, you'll be able to go see your little sister again."

Caleb sat there silently digesting what he had just heard. Walt and Heather were silent as well both wondering when and if they should add anything else.

Finally, breaking the silence, Caleb looked up and said, "Okay."

Heather slipped into the kitchen and returned with a slice of cake for the boy. He nodded a thank you and slowly began to ingest the treat.

Walt broke the silence, "Hey I know what we should do! Let's stop by *Waffle World* and have breakfast on the way. You know how you like their waffles with ice cream." This brought a small smile to Caleb who nodded and said, "Okay."

The next day, after a stop at *Waffle World* the family jumped into the car and headed for the hospital. Walt and Heather talked casually, and Caleb said little as he stared out the window. After visiting little Sarah, they went downstairs where a sample of Caleb's blood would be drawn. Walt sat there holding his hand while Heather stroked his blond hair. Other than wincing a bit, the boy emitted little reaction. The doctor commented on how brave he was and told the parents that he should be able to give them some information by the next day.

Before dinner the following day, Walt called Caleb in from the back yard. He ushered him into the living room and asked him to have a seat. Heather joined her son on the couch.

"Caleb, we got some really good news today" Walt began. "It looks like your blood is a perfect match for Sarah. The doctors say that if you give your blood to Sarah, she has a really good chance of living."

Caleb glanced from Walt to Heather. He looked down and seemed to be fighting tears. Walt and Heather let their son take it in. But then they were surprised when Caleb quietly said, "I don't want to do it."

"But Caleb, if you don't give her your blood, she won't be able to live" his mother said.

Caleb sat their silently as if he was trying to figure it all out. Neither Walt nor Heather were prepared for his reaction, and both were unsure what to say. Then Caleb slid off the couch and headed toward his room. Then he stopped and without turning around said,

"I don't want to do it. Please don't make me do it!"

Walt and Heather sat on the couch dumbfounded. The silence

was broken by the loud sound of Caleb's bedroom door slamming shut. The two of them looked at each other as the tears began to slide from Heather's eyes.

Later that night, as they both put their son to bed Walt knelt beside Caleb and said, "Son, I know you're scared. I would be too. But this is something that Sarah needs. She needs your blood. Now you're going to have to be brave and do the right thing." Then stroking his head, he said, "I know you'll do what's right. And your little sister will be so thankful to you." Caleb fought back a tear and nodded his head.

The next day Caleb came into the kitchen and went right to Heather. He put his arms around her and pressed his head into her side. She returned the hug and smiled when he said, "I'm ready. I'll give her my blood."

"I'm so proud of you" she said and kissed the top of his head.

Late that afternoon Caleb and his parents were in the transfusion room at the hospital. Little Sarah was prepped and wrapped up tightly and lying in a bassinet next to Caleb's bed. Both Walt and Heather kissed Caleb and helped him up on the bed. The doctor began prepping his arm for his I. V.

When the needle was inserted into his arm and connected to Sarah's the love Caleb had for his sister was revealed.

With tears fighting to escape his eyes, he asked the doctor, "Am I going to die now?" The doctor cleared the boy's confusion while the tears poured from his parents' eyes. They spent the rest of the time smothering him with hugs, kisses, and assuring words of comfort and love.

(Adapted from Chicken Soup for the Soul-1993)

-29-
KINDNESS CHOSEN

Early one Saturday morning, Dr. Kenneth Parker was seated in his favorite coffee shop enjoying both a caramel latte and the company of four seminary students. He had been a professor at the seminary for over twelve years and was often found in the store. It was very common to find him sitting and talking with students from the seminary especially when he showed up in the early mornings.

The subjects they covered ranged from theology to philosophy and even sports. He loved being around the students and felt that it was one of the things that kept the sixty-two-year-old young and energetic. Quite often their talks started with a question from a student and moved into a large cup of information about the particular topic. Dr. Parker had a way of communicating which was both deep and endearing but laced with gentleness. The students never felt demeaned but always edified and hungry for more time with the man.

On this particular Saturday the students sat in rapt attention as he shared ideas about creation and even wove in an illustration from sports. Bits of laughter and times of head nodding were common reactions from those in the circle.

At one point, another professor and friend of Kenneth's came by the table with a couple of to-go cups. He nudged Dr. Parker who stood and shared a short hug and a smile. The two exchanged their plans for the day and the visitor excused himself saying that his wife was waiting in the car. The man left by saying, "Have a great day Tip!"

When Dr. Parker sat back down, one of the students asked him, "Did he just call you Tip?"

"Yes" he said. "It's sort of a nickname I got several years ago."

"What's it mean?" another asked.

"Well" he responded slowly. "It's Short for tipo, and in Spanish it means kindness. A student from Mexico hung it on me about ten years ago."

"I can see that" one of the boys quipped. You're one of the kindest men I've ever met.

He slowly shook his head and said, "Well it hasn't always been that way."

"Yeah right" another student chuckled.

"No, I'm afraid it's true." He countered as he shrugged his shoulders.

"See, I've always been a very serious teacher-still am. But back then I was not only serious, but I was abrupt and a very no-nonsense kind of guy. I didn't have much patience with anyone who didn't take things as seriously as I did, and I didn't have much tolerance for those who were late or those who weren't paying attention."

The students looked puzzled as he continued.

"But that all changed on one day. I was teaching a class on Systematic Theology and there was a student named Anthony. I still remember his name.

He fell asleep at almost the exact time every day." The students nodded and leaned forward.

"Well, one day, I guess I was in a bad mood, but at the end of the class I asked a nearby student to wake him up. When he awoke, I said, 'Mr. Addison, if you can't stay awake in my class, don't come back until you can."

A collective sigh could be heard from the group.

"As the class was filing out, a student came up to me and said, 'Dr. Parker, I wish you wouldn't have said that to Anthony. You see, his wife is in the hospital with cancer. He spends the entire night with her, goes to work for a few hours and then races over here for class. He's got it really tough.'" Dr. Parker paused to see the effect his story was having on the group.

"His words never left my head for the entire day. That night I went for a long walk. I walked and I prayed. I prayed and I walked.

The man who came home was a different man."

The students nodded in silence and unison.

"Beyond that, I began putting real value in the opportunity to be kind." I realized that when you're right, you turn heads, but when you're kind, you turn hearts. And turned hearts last longer than turned heads. When you're right you win arguments. But when you're kind, you win friends." The professor waited to let everything sink in.

"So that was a defining moment for me. And it's why I try to be nice to everybody. Because I understand that I don't know their whole story, but I know that it seems like everybody is having a hard time."

"So that's how I got the nickname Tipo or Tip. Any questions?

One of the students spoke for the group. "No questions. It all makes total sense. Thanks for sharing that with us."

"My pleasure. Well, I gotta get going. Got a few things to do at the house today." With that, he stood up, nodded to the group, tossed his coffee cup in the trash and moved toward the door.

The students shouted after him, "Thanks Dr. Parker!"

When he left the students looked at one another smiling. One of them broke the ice by saying "Tip." The group nodded together and one of them said, "Makes perfect sense."

Then the young men left with a clear understanding that they had gotten a life-long lesson making them both smarter and better. A lesson one can't buy but can only learn in the classroom of life.

-30-
THE TEST OF COMMITMENT

After 42 years of marriage, Robert still loved his wife deeply. They had been through the normal and sometimes abnormal ups and downs of married life. They raised their five children to adulthood, moved several times, and worked their way up the educational ladder. Their professional climb reached its zenith when Robert became the President of Columbia Bible College and Seminary in Columbia, S.C. He served CBC for 22 years and enjoyed a positive relationship with both the trustees as well as the faculty and students. Life was easily labeled *good* by Robert and Muriel McQuilken.

But then life began to turn for them. Robert began to notice some changes in Muriel. She began to forget things like friends' names and even the names of family members. Sometimes she would say things completely out of place and put things in places where they didn't belong. Twice she left the stove on, and several times she put refrigerated items in the oven. A few times she entered the living room with only one sock on or two different shoes.

Robert was as confused about Muriel as she was about herself and a trip to a specialist was called for. With guidance from friends, Robert made the appointment with no objection from Muriel.

After running a few tests, it was confirmed that Muriel was suffering from the early stages of Alzheimer's disease. Medications, diet changes and exercises were prescribed. She was to be watched and the doctor informed of the effects of these measures.

Things seemed to be getting slightly better. Although Muriel began to speak less and less, her behavior looked like it was improving, and the couple were both prayerful and hopeful. Even her sense of humor began to return.

One day, during a commercial break, she asked Robert, "How come dinosaurs can't talk?"

Robert was taken aback by the obscure question but responded suspecting that it was a joke or riddle. "I have no idea."

Muriel turned to him and said, "Because they're all dead." With that she smiled, nodded, and turned back to the T.V. Robert chuckled and gently shook his head.

But about a year later, things started to rapidly decline for Muriel and likewise for Robert. Her appetite dropped off, sleep fled from her, and she became fearful for no apparent reason. She was particularly anxious when Robert was not in the room and would often call out to him until he returned. The doctor's evaluation revealed that the disease was progressing faster than anticipated and he recommended outside help and a change in medication.

All this led to Robert's announcement during a weekly student and faculty gathering in the campus chapel. With his emotions running as high as the chapel's vaulted ceiling, Robert stood before those gathered, so many of which he had grown to know and love.

After a few preliminary comments, Robert grasped the edges of the podium and explained the condition that he and Muriel were facing. He cleared his throat and said, "The decision was made, in a way, 42 years ago when I promised to care for Muriel 'in sickness and in health....till death do us part.' So, as a man of my word, integrity has something to do with it. But so does fairness. Muriel has cared for me fully and sacrificially all these years; if I cared for her for the next 40 years I would not be out of debt. Duty, however, can be grim and stoic. But there is more; I love Muriel. She is a delight to me – her childlike dependence and confidence in me, her warm love, occasional flashes of that wit that I used to relish so, her happy spirit and tough resilience in the face of her continually distressing frustration. I do not have to care for her, I get to. It is a high honor to care for so wonderful a person. So, with our situation being what it is, I feel that God would have me spend my time with my wife and I will be resigning my position effective at the end of the month. Thank you for all your support and prayers and may God bless you and this great institution."

With that, the students rose in unison and applause. Robert began the long walk up the aisle with students blocking his way with hugs, pats on the back, and words of encouragement. And Robert McQuilken went home and fulfilled the promise he made over 42 years ago to the love of his life.

(Adapted from Robertson McQuilken's resignation speech.)

-31-
THE HEART OF ADOPTION

Sheri and Tracey were close friends. They had met during their sophomore year in college and stayed close ever since. Coffee, lunch outings, and even picnics in the park were all part of the activities that gave them an excuse to spend time together. The friendship that their daughters developed made their relational bond even stronger.

Sheri and her husband Mike always wanted children but were unable to conceive and after three years of marriage they began looking into adopting a baby. They went through all the procedures and eagerly waited for the day when they would have a child in their hearts and home. And Tracey and her husband Darren walked with Sheri and Mike as they went through the adoption process. This resulted in Maddie becoming their daughter over six years ago.

Mike and Sheri were blessed to be able to adopt Maddie while she was still being carried by her birth mother. They traveled over 600 miles to be in the delivery room when she was born and two days later were able to take her home from the hospital.

They were committed to being good parents and were reward-ed with a young girl who filled their home with love and laughter. Though not perfect, Maddie was proving to be a blessing in every sense of the word. She was bright and compliant and had a face that broke out in a smile at the slightest hint of anything that tugged at her heart.

Sheri and Mike never hid from Maddie the fact that she was adopted. They used words like *chosen*, *blessing*, and *gift* when describing how she came to be such an integral part of their family. And up to this point Maddie never questioned their love for her and never really asked why her *birth mom* put her up for adoption.

Maddie's understanding of adoption was explained to Sheri one morning when the two ladies took their children to a nearby fast-food restaurant. Having finished their breakfast, the girls went into the play area while Sheri and Tracey stayed at the table and enjoyed an extra cup of coffee.

"I gotta tell you something" Tracey leaned forward and said.

Sheri matched her movement, "Whatcha got?"

"That daughter of yours is something else" Tracey began nodding her head in the direction of the play area.

"I know" Sheri said with a slight smile.

"After you dropped Maddie off and headed to the dentist, I gave the girls a snack and set them down to watch a little T.V."

Sheri nodded.

"Well, somehow the topic of adoption came up in the show they were glued to. I heard Riley ask Maddie, what's 'doption?" she said as she put her hands up making quotation marks in the air.

This brought a slight grin and nod from Sheri.

"I'll never forget what your sweet daughter said."

Sheri's head turned slightly to the side as she leaned further in. "Well, are you gonna tell me, or should I start guessing?"

A broad smile came to Tracey's face. "She said, 'doption is when a Mommy carries a baby in her heart instead of her tummy'"

With that, both ladies turned to the play area and smiled.

"So much wisdom" Sheri said quietly.

Tracey nodded and offered, "And truth."

Sheri breathed deeply and said, "Out of the mouths of babes."

Both ladies gave the smile of women who understood their blessings.

-32-
THE UNWRAPPED STORY

They were only ten years old but certainly should have known better. Sammy and his buddy Perry bounced into the living room with an imitation limp followed by laughter. Sammy's father Marcus and his neighbor George were seated at the kitchen table sorting out screws that George needed for a home project.

When the boys came in Marcus asked them, "What's so funny fellas?"

The boys got quiet, but Sammy's father asked again, "C'mon guys. Tell us what you're laughing at."

Sammy answered tentatively, "Nothin.' We just saw Cripp around the corner."

"Who?"

"A guy everybody calls Cripp. He lives around the corner. We saw him walking across his lawn."

George asked, "Why do you call him Cripp?"

"Cause he walks funny. Like he's crippled" Perry said.

"Do you mean the tall skinny guy with the shriveled hand?" Marcus asked.

"Yeah. That's him" Sammy answered. "We didn't mean nothin' by it. He just looks funny when he walks."

Marcus looked at George, gave a small sigh and told the boys, "You guys need to come over here and sit down."

The boys obeyed both sensing they were in at least a minor amount of trouble.

Marcus gazed at one boy and then the other. "Listen guys" he said. "There's something about Mr. Dyer, that's his real name, that you don't know. Mr. Dyer's daughter and her husband lived a couple of towns away. A couple of years after they got married, they had a baby boy named Alex. When Alex was about four months old, they asked Mr. Dyer if he would come over and babysit so they could go out to dinner."

The faces of both boys showed they were paying attention.

"Mr. Dyer watched over his grandson for about an hour when a big storm came up. The rain came pouring down in sheets and the wind was howling. It was a huge storm. Trees began to fall everywhere, and the power was out. When Alex's parents came home, they were shocked to see a gigantic tree had fallen on their house."

The boys' brows were visibly furrowed.

George picked up the story. "When they went inside, they found that the tree had gone straight through the roof of Alex's room. They panicked! They had to break branches and climb through limbs to get to their son. When they got to his crib, they found Mr. Dyer laying on top of it shielding his grandson."

Both boys gently nodded their heads.

Marcus spoke, "He was alive, but he was in bad shape." They called 911 and the rescue workers had to use a chain saw to get him out. The baby was unhurt. but Mr. Dyer was in critical condition and needed surgery. The tree had injured his spine which is why he limps, and his arm is twisted up."

Both boys were visibly ashamed. They looked down at the table without saying a word. Finally, Perry spoke up. "We didn't know that! Honest!" "Yeah, we never heard that story before" Sammy added.

George spoke up, "And you know Coach Kennedy from the high school football team?" Both boys nodded. "Well, that's Mr. Dyer's grandson Alex." Mr. Dyer can't move well because he protected Coach Kennedy when he was a little baby."

Marcus spoke gently yet directly, "Now I don't ever want to hear you guys making fun of him again. And you can tell your buddies that goes for them too. Anybody that does what he did for his grandson deserves nothing but respect."

The boys nodded and Sammy quietly added, "Yes Sir."

"Now I want you two to do something for me. Actually, it's more for you. Your mom made some chocolate chip cookies. They're on the counter. I want you guys to each take one and enjoy it." Both boys looked at the counter while trying not to smile. "While you're bringing several to Mr. Dyer's house."

George nodded in agreement.

"Really?" Sammy said. "Do we have to?"

"Yes. You have to."

Marcus got up and put six cookies in a plastic bag. "Now just go over there, tell him your mom made these and that your family hopes he has a good day."

Sammy could tell by the look on his dad's face that there was no point in either arguing or resisting and minutes later he and Perry were knocking on the door of Mr. Dyer's house.

And from that day on, they only greeted Mr. Dyer with respect and admiration. They learned a valuable lesson they carried with them for the rest of their lives even passing it on to their children. "Don't be quick to criticize someone. You may not know their story."

-33-
CRUMBS OF HOPE

Dennis didn't want to be there. None of the guys did. But duty and the draft called him to Vietnam. So, he left his home and family in Gainesville, Florida on a hot June morning and boarded a bus for Fayetteville, North Carolina.

He was normally an early riser and in relatively good shape going into the service, so he didn't struggle as much as some of the other guys. He worked hard knowing that his life and the lives of those around him depended on him paying attention and being responsible.

When boot camp was over, he and his new comrades jumped on a plane and headed to a land seemingly millions of miles away. They landed in Da Nang, checked in with the commanding officer, and got ready to engage in the assigned tasks. Growing up in Florida, Dennis was used hot days. But his days in Vietnam were of a heat on a different level. The burning sun seemed relentless. The only reprieve from the heat was the long periods of rain. A regular comment was that if the sun doesn't melt you, the rain will drown you.

Dennis and his company spent two or three nights at a time on patrol. They covered several miles occasionally encountering enemy fire. Discomfort and fatigue became his constant companions. One day his buddy stepped on a hidden board with spikes in it while they crossed a narrow stream. His foot quickly became infected requiring surgery, and he was sent to the MASH unit for the procedure. This put Dennis constantly on edge.

So much of what his unit did seemed like a waste of time to Dennis. They'd battle and take a hill only to give it back two days later. They'd drive the enemy out of a village and have to return the following week to do the very same thing.

Dennis missed his home and family to painful levels. All he focused on was doing his job, staying alive, and counting down the days until he was homeward bound. His days were filled with grueling tasks and his nights were filled with memories of friends and family in Gainesville.

With just a month left in his service time, he was ordered to board a helicopter and head to a combat zone. A foreboding sense came over his entire body and seated itself in his brain. He wasn't sure which brought more fear, battling the enemy or riding in a copter. But orders were orders and Dennis dutifully climbed aboard stuffing himself between two other soldiers to go who knows where and encounter who knows what.

The copter jumped off the ground, turned 180 degrees, angled its nose down and its tail up and went flashing into the heart of the country. The trip wasn't far but to Dennis it seemed endless. The noise from the helicopter was so loud that even the shouts of the men nearby went largely unheard. But the sound of enemy fire was unmistakable.

Bullets ripped through the side of the copter injuring two of the men sitting close to Dennis. The men returned fire unsure of where to direct the lead. In a flash, Dennis felt the copter spin out of control and knew they had been hit by something big. Several men screamed and a single voice from the pilot was heard, "Hold on!"

Moments later the aircraft was on its' side and in flames. The impact caused the death of several of the men and Dennis felt pain throughout his entire body. He tried to lift his right arm, but it wouldn't move. He had a man under him and one lying on top of him. He didn't know if they were dead or alive. He only knew that he had to get out of there. He used his good arm and both legs to free himself from the men and the flaming helicopter, then rolled free of the aircraft.

He pressed himself to his feet noting his throbbing head and the loud buzz in his ears. When he looked to his left, he saw one of the men stagger from behind the copter and made a move to join him.

It was then that he felt a hand on his collar, pulling him backward and slamming him to the ground. He turned his head slightly and met the end of a rifle. A black boot struck his face forcing Dennis to fight for consciousness. Moments later his hands were bound and he was jerked to his feet. All around him enemy soldiers were screaming things at him he couldn't understand. Several of them punched him in the face and chest.

With a gun's muzzle constantly pressing into his back he was pushed toward a large village. He had lost sight of the other soldier and could only assume that he was alone. Several times he stumbled and fell only to be snatched from the ground and struck in the back of his head. He looked at his right arm and saw the gash that caused the loss of use. He could feel the blood running down his arm and soaking his hand and sleeve. He knew he needed medical help.

A short time later, he was pressed into the village. There he found a mob of angry people yelling more things at him that he couldn't understand. They threw rocks and sand at him. They shook their fists at him and spit on him. Dennis was unsure if he would die from the wound on his arm, the bullets from the soldiers, or the anger of the mob. Hope was quickly evaporating.

Then something very strange and unique happened. A little woman who looked to be about 70 years of age stood in front of him. She reached behind him and found his bound hands. He felt her squeeze something into his left hand and step back in front of him. Then she made the sign of the cross, pressed her hands together and slightly bowed. Seconds later she was pressed into the crowd by one of the soldiers.

A half-hour later, Dennis was slammed into a small hut that was to be his quarters for the next four months. When his wrists were untied, he strained to open his left hand. There he found a small piece of crushed bread. It was not enough to sustain life, but the bread and that gesture from the old woman was enough to birth hope in his heart. And until his release that was the image that sustained him.

-34-
THE ART OF SACRIFICE

The year was 1490. On a park bench on the edge of a small river in Nuremberg Germany, two friends, Albrect Durer, and Franz Knigstein sat discussing their futures as well as their options.

Albrect said, "It's quite obvious that we can't keep going on like this. It's not possible for us to work the way we do while pursuing our passion in the world of art.

"You are right my friend," said Franz. "You are much too gifted to waste away at the goldsmiths."

"You are just as gifted as I Franz!" Albrect countered, "and just as wasteful of the gift the Lord has given you."

"What is it that we are to do?" Franz asked. "We must work if we are to eat but studying under Michael Wolgemut has a price to it as well."

The young men sat in silence watching the slow-moving river for several minutes.

Franz finally spoke up. "I know what we must do! One of us must go into the apprenticeship with Master Wolgemut while the other one will work to pay for the costs. Then after learning what he must learn to be great, he will come back and support the other one in his apprenticeship."

Albrect turned to his friend, "That is a great idea. But how will we decide who will go first?"

"We'll draw lots." Franz said. That's the fairest way. Whoever the lot falls to will go into the apprenticeship first."

"Good idea" Albrect said. With that he pulled four coins from his pocket.

Each coin was of the same type but carried a different date. "The oldest coin drawn will be the winner." He put the coins in his small pouch and pushed it toward his friend. "You draw first."

Franz reached two fingers into the pouch and pulled out a coin. "1486" he said showing it to Al.

Albrect reached in the pouch pulling out his coin. He looked at it and wrapped it in his palm putting his hand on his lap.

"Well," said Franz. "Hand it over."

Albrect reached toward his friend and dropped the coin in his hand. Franz looked at the date, "1484" he said with slight grin. "It's settled then. You will apprentice under Michael Wolgemut and I will work and earn what we need."

Albrect looked at Franz, "Are you sure about this?"

Franz nodded and said, "I am sure my friend. Just as I am sure that in a short time, you will be labeled great amongst the artists of Germany."

And so it began, two friends bent on helping one another reach their dreams.

Two days later, Al left to sit under the wings and will of Wolgemut one of Germany's finest artists. And Franz headed to the goldsmith, working with his hands in an entirely different fashion.

The next three years went by quickly. The boys kept in touch with one another through letters and an occasional visit by Al. Franz worked long and hard at the goldsmith's hauling ore and pounding metal.

Meanwhile Albrect, like a sponge, learned and grew as an artist. All Nuremberg, as well as so many others who viewed his work, recognized the divine talent this young man had as an artist. Before long, his sketches and carvings were featured in some of Germany's finest artistic gatherings and presentations and as he traveled through many of the cities of Europe many began to consider him an artistic genius.

The time came for the boys to complete their agreement and switch places. When Albrect returned to Nuremberg he was greeted by Franz with open arms. But although the arms were open, the hands of his friend were in a physical way closed. Through a combination of a hug and handshake, Albrect noted that Franz' hands had become hard and calloused. His fingers were thick and scarred and Franz grimaced slightly at Albrect's handshake. It was evident that the years of hard labor had taken their toll on his friend's hands. He had lost his subtle and delicate touch that are mandated in the world of art. Arthritis had set in and several of his fingers had become stiff and somewhat twisted.

Franz showed no signs of resentment toward his friend, but rather rejoiced in the climb he had made in the world of art. Albrect had become extremely well known and Franz celebrated his success. Although his days in the world of fine art had come to an end, he reveled in his close relationship with a man who was to become one of Germany's finest artists.

All these emotions were evidenced one day when Albrect came to visit his old friend. He knocked on the door and when no one answered he entered Franz' house. He called to Franz but got no reply. Upon walking to the back room, he found his friend on his knees in the middle of a time of prayer. Franz was leaning on the edge of a chair with his hands clasped and his forehead resting on the back of his knuckles.

Albrect stood in the hall and heard through the partially opened door, a prayer that he would never forget.

"...And heavenly Father, I know that you have deeply blessed Albrect with wisdom and talent unlike anyone else. Thank you for touching both his mind and his hands. I ask you to keep your hand strong in his life and go with him every step as he continues in the world in which you have placed him..."

Albrect stepped back fighting tears. The image of his friend was forever etched in his mind. He stepped into the other room and drew a small pad from his coat pocket. With the stub of a pencil, he quickly sketched a picture of Franz' gnarled hands clasped in prayer.

Later, while sitting on the same bench he had frequented with his friend, Albrect completed a masterpiece known as *The Praying Hands.* Today art galleries around the world feature Albrecht Durer's remarkable talent, and this particular piece tells an amazing story of friendship and sacrifice.

-35-
LIFE-GIVING SACRIFICE

James stepped out of the January cold and into his house only to find his wife Krystal sitting on their couch wiping away tears. He slid his laptop onto the side table, slipped off his coat, and raced over to her dropping down by her side. "What's wrong Babe?"

"Nothing's wrong!" she replied pulling another tissue from the box. "In fact, everything is great, just perfect."

James sat down next to her. "Honey, tell me what's going on."

Krystal sniffed, "You know how I went to the clinic last week to have my blood checked to see if I could be a match for Pastor Jenning's kidney transplant?"

"Yeah, of course I do" James said pulling her close. "You're not a match?"

"Yes, I am" she said as a new set of tears began. "The clinic called about twenty minutes ago and told me I'm a perfect match."

James leaned toward her and asked, "So why the tears?"

I'm a perfect match and I'm a thankful match. But I'm a terrified thankful perfect match."

James pulled her even closer. "I don't blame you for being scared. The doctor did say that it would be painful. But he also told us that he'd done over one-hundred of these transplants with great success for the donor and the recipient. We prayed about it, and I believe it's gonna be okay."

Krystal nodded putting her head on his shoulder. "And Pastor Jenning has got to have a new kidney" she said quietly.

"Yes" James added. "He can't survive without it."

Shortly after moving to Wisconsin, James and Krystal had become close friends with the Jennings. Besides church activities, the two families spent time at one another's house playing card games and watching movies. Their children became good friends and the two couples even double dated on a regular basis. They were friends, good friends.

But when Andrew started having pain in his back and blood in his urine a series of tests revealed that he was suffering from 20% failure in one kidney and 80% failure in the other. For six months he endured dialysis and the procedure seemed to help quite a bit. But the effectiveness of this treatment began to wane. His one kidney was no longer functioning, and the other was only working at 40% capacity. Drastic measures were called for. A kidney transplant was in order.

Surgery was scheduled as soon as the results of Krystal's blood work were delivered to Andrew's doctor. Krystal was given several medications as well as a strict diet. When word reached the church body, intense prayers were offered up both for Pastor Jennings as well as Krystal.

The day of the surgery came quickly. A prayer vigil was held at the church and the hospital parking lot held several members with large posters of encouragement. Pastor Jennings had spent the night in the hospital, but Krystal and James arrived a few hours before surgery. As they drove up, they were met with cheers, hugs, and pats on the back.

After the initial prepping, Krystal was wheeled into the surgery room. Pastor Jennings was already there along with both teams for the double surgery.

With a confident voice he said to Krystal, "I know I told you this before, but you will never know how thankful I am for you. God bless you!

"He has" she replied.

Then Pastor Jennings extended his hand toward her, and she met his hand in the middle of the gurneys. "Let's pray" he said. Krystal nodded.

"Dear Father, thank you for our friendship and thank you for your love. At this time, we pray for strength for Krystal and myself and wisdom for those performing this procedure. In Jesus name, amen."

"Amen" Krystal along with many in the room repeated. Then disguising her fear, Krystal said softly, "We always wanted a pastor we could be close to, but I didn't think it would be this close." Andrew smiled broadly and nodded toward Krystal, then toward the staff signifying that they were both ready to begin the surgery.

Four hours later, a groggy Krystal and Andrew were wheeled to the recovery room where their spouses waited. Their beds were separated only by a curtain. They were both heavily sedated and appeared to be pain free.

Before too long, Andrew called out to Krystal, "Hey Krystal, you okay?"

"Yeah, I'm fine" she said weakly. "Just a little sleepy."

"Any pain?" he asked.

"No, I don't think so" she replied. "How about you?"

"I think I'm good. I'm a little scared to move."

"Well, I have to tell you, I was very scared the whole time. I guess I need to work on my faith a little."

"Yeah, I guess so" he said. "I wasn't worried a bit. In fact, I slept through the entire process."

The patients and their spouses all chuckled a bit.

Through their time of recovery, the families continued to support and encourage each other. The years of their friendship continued to grow and both Krystal and her pastor lived for many years enjoying sound health and increased faith.

-36-
THE SECURITY OF KINDNESS

"They say she'll grow out of it. But I have my doubts" Joanie thought as she lifted Meagan from her car seat. "If this is a security blanket, I think I have a very insecure little girl on my hands."

Joannie and her three-year-old daughter had been running errands and had stopped for a bite of lunch. They'd been to the grocery store, the post office, the thrift store, and now the diner. When her feet hit the ground, Meagan was quick to grab her little blanket, put her thumb in her mouth, and reach for her momma's hand.

There wasn't much of a blanket left after tears, stains, and food residue had had their way with the fabric. Joannie had kept the cloth clean but had to cut it several times because of the holes and marks. Secretly she thought there would come a day when the blanket would become too small even for Meagan's little hands.

Meagan was a good little girl and seemed to carry a very compliant disposition. But all that changed in an instant at the slightest suggestion that she leave her *blankie* behind. The two went everywhere together including church, the playground, and even rides on her tricycle. Joannie tried to be patient, but there were times when she was tempted to throw out what remained of the blanket and endure the wrath of a three-year-old. But Meagan's distressed face and the assurance from friends and family that she would grow out of it, always put Joannie's plans to rest. So, with her usual sigh, she escorted Meagan, and her blankie across the parking lot and toward the diner.

Just before reaching their seats, Joannie drew Meagan's attention to a basinet cradling a sleeping infant girl. "Look Meagan! Isn't she adorable?" The mother of the little one broke out in a prideful smile. "She's so little" Meagan said. "You were that size once too you know" Joannie said. "Yes, But I'm big now" Meagan countered. After gazing at the little girl for a few moments, the two made their way to a booth for a short lunch.

After lunch the two headed for the car. It wasn't until she lifted Meagan up to her car seat that Joannie notice that her blanket was missing. She quickly looked on the floor, and on the ground, but saw no sign of the fabric of security. She looked at Meagan and was surprised that no panic was resting on her face. She asked her daughter, "Meagan, where's your blanket?" Returning her gaze Meaghan said in a matter-of-fact way, "That baby in the food place didn't have one. And all babies need a blankie, so I gave her mine."

And with a smile and a short nod, Joannie realized that her friends and family were right. Her little girl had grown out of needing her blanket and had taken a step toward maturity and security. A celebration was called for, so the two stopped for a mandatory scoop of ice cream before heading home to report this long-awaited landmark event to Meagan's dad.

-37-
THE FREEDOM OF KINDNESS

Dean Arlington was known for two things: He was an accomplished state senator, and he was an outspoken Christian. So, it surprised no one when he accepted a request from a prison ministry to address the inmates from the state penitentiary.

Senator Arlington spoke to over 200 inmates gathered in the prison's auditorium. Afterward he asked the warden if he and his team could visit the men on death row. Because a prisoner was recently executed, things were tense there, but the warden reluctantly agreed.

Senator Arlington actually knew two of the inmates on death row and had been corresponding with each of them over the last year. When he and his team arrived, the warden opened the individual doors and the men slowly walked to a designated meeting area where Arlington and his twenty volunteers had gathered.

Death row was quite different from the rest of the prison. Although the entire prison was "maximum security," death row carried a feeling of a higher level of security. All the cells were separated by double rows of iron bars, and each cell opened individually. There was an air about that cell block that is hard to describe. But the heaviness and gloom in the atmosphere gave one a surreal feeling. One might say that the fingers of death were wrapped tightly around the entire area.

Each of the men on death row were found guilty of crimes that were punishable by death. Some of them had been confined there for years as appeals for new trials came. Many of them looked as if they had already been executed.

The inmates paired off with the volunteers. Names were exchanged, handshakes were offered, and Bibles were opened. Senator Arlington spent his time talking with the two men he knew and ended their time praying over them.

Later that day the Senator was scheduled to meet with the Governor of a nearby state and knew that a plane was waiting for him at a private airport. So, he called out to the volunteers and the men wrapped up their time with prayer. Then all those gathered including the inmates joined together and sang *Amazing Grace* after which they all said their good-byes and the volunteers began filing out.

When the volunteers were all gathered in a separate area, they noticed that one of the men in their group was missing. The Senator returned to the block and found John Clement holding an open Bible and sharing some scripture with a man.

Senator Arlington told John that they had to go, and that the warden was anxious to close the man's cell and then close the double gates between death row and the rest of the prison.

"Mr. Clement, it's time to go" the Senator said. "The warden has to close the gates to this area, and he can't do it until we leave."

"Just a few more minutes" John said. "This is important."

"I'm sorry, but we have to go now!" Senator Arlington said with a little sternness to his voice. "I have an appointment with a Governor, and I can't keep him waiting."

John turned to the Senator and in a low voice said, "Senator, this is very important. You see, I'm Judge Clement. I'm the man who sentenced James here to die. But now he's my brother and we want a minute to pray together."

The Senator nodded his head and gave a look of understanding. He stepped away from the men, and quietly said, "I see. Take your time. The Governor can wait."

(Adapted from *Loving God* by Chuck Colson)

-38-
KINDNESS IN CLEATS

Ronnie lived alone in a good-sized house on the outskirts of Dallas. He was an accomplished investment counselor with a small firm in the city. He was both a good brother and proud uncle. He loved it when his sister Maria came by and enjoyed his time with his nephew and niece. Dotti and Drew were eight-year-old twins and they loved seeing their uncle and reveled in the way he spoiled them with treats. That Saturday morning the three of them stopped by to see Ronnie on their way to drop off some food at a friend's house. When Ronnie learned of their coming, he made sure to stock up on lunch meats, ice cream, and small bags of candy for their trip.

As he and Maria sat enjoying a cup of coffee, the two young ones spent their time exploring his large back yard. He had a horseshoe pit, a cornhole set, a basketball goal, a hammock, and several trees perfectly branched for climbing. Every now and then they would slip up to the porch and grab a cookie before checking out something else in Ronnie's back yard.

Ronnie had a new painting he wanted to show Maria, so he escorted her downstairs to his home office. The room was filled with typical office supplies and his desk though orderly was covered with files and charts. He was showing her the waterfall painting when the twins bounced in.

They enjoyed the painting as well but became quickly enamored by his trophies, sports pictures, and memorabilia. Ronnie had been a successful athlete. He played football and basketball in high school and football in college. As a linebacker, he started his last two years at North Dallas University where his success earned him a try out for the Philadelphia Eagles. When he didn't make the team, he moved his skills into the business world.

The children were captivated by all his awards and asked if they could hold several of them. They had questions about so many of them and Ronnie patiently told a story connected to each one.

Then Drew pointed to a football on the top shelf and asked about it. Ronnie reached up and pulled it down. In white marker on the side of it was the score:

N. Dallas 23

Houston Central 20

The other side held the signature Calvin Huntington

Ronnie sat down in his chair and the kids leaned into him. They knew the details were on the way.

"The Houston Central Cardinals were one of our big rivals. We didn't like those guys and they didn't like us. By my senior year, we had only beaten them one time, so we were hungry for a win. We weren't having a great season, but we had won five games. The game with the Cardinals was the last game of the season and my last game in college." Both children gave a nod of understanding.

Ronnie tossed the ball up a couple of times and then continued, "With two minutes to go, they were beating us by four points. They had the ball and were driving down the field. It looked like at the very least they were gonna' get a field goal. They got down to our 37 and it was third and five."

Drew leaned into his sister and said, "That means it was third down and five yards to go for a first."

"I know that," she said following it with a heavy sigh.

Shaking the ball with his one hand Uncle Ronnie said, "Well, the quarterback dropped back to pass, we blitz the other linebacker, and I dropped back in coverage. The ball came over my head and I jumped up and touched it. I fell on my back and didn't know what happened, but the crowd was going nuts. I rolled over to see our corner with the ball."

Both children couldn't contain themselves.

"Then what happened?" Dotti asked.

Drew jumped in and said, "Yea, what happened next?"

"Well," Ronnie continued, "The corner caught the ball and was running right passed me. I got up on my feet and started running down the sideline right behind him."

Ronnie's voice revealed his excitement. "We crossed the fifty, the forty, the thirty. There was no one around and he was gonna score! I kept running behind him yelling the whole time, Go Cal! Go Cal!"

"Who's Cal?" Drew asked.

"That was his name. His name was Calvin, but we called him Cal."

"Like on the football!" Dotti said pointing to the signature.

"That's right" Ronnie said, poking her in the stomach with the tip of the ball.

"But then when he got to the twenty-yard line, he slowed down and I caught up with him. I kept yelling the whole time and you wouldn't believe what happened next."

Drew leaned on Ronnie's knee and asked, "What?"

"He kept running but he turned to me and handed me the ball. I took it and ran the rest of the way into the end zone. I scored the touchdown, and we won the game!"

"Wow! That's a cool story Uncle Ron!" Drew said.

Dotti added, "Yeah! You were a hero that day."

Ronnie smiled and said, "Well kinda. But as far as I'm concerned, the real hero that day was Calvin Huntington. He did something he didn't have to do, and I'll never forget him for it."

"He was a good guy, wasn't he?" Drew said.

"The best," Ronnie countered. "And you know, out of all the trophies and awards in this room, this is my absolute favorite. This ball is my friendship trophy and I'll never forget what Cal did that day."

And while Maria drove to the rest of their errands, she smiled as the children repeated so many of the parts of that story. Later the children called Ronnie and told him that they decided that the name of that story should be called *Kindness in Cleats*. Ronnie agreed and from that day on he always prefaced the story with that title.

-39-
LOVE BEYOND THE PAIN

Groggy doesn't describe how Marcus felt. He lay heavily sedated in a hospital bed overnight. As he opened his eyes, he felt a hand on his forearm and before he could focus, he knew that it was the loving hand of Gina.

But when his eyes finally cooperated with his mind, he found that the hand belonged to Mr. Phil Pettigrove. Marcus was surprised but did his best not to show it. He wasn't sure where he was and had an even lesser sense of how he got there.

Phil broke the silence by quietly saying, "Hey Marcus. How ya doing?"

"Not sure," Marcus said in a whisper. "Where am I?"

"You're in the hospital. You've gotten quite a beating, but the doctors say you'll be okay."

He explained to him that Gina had spent the night but had just left a couple of hours ago. He told him that she would return after she showered and changed her clothes.

Marcus tried to move but felt pain in his head, chest, and a few other places.

Phil spoke again, "Try to lay still son. You've got a couple of broken ribs and a concussion."

Reality started creeping into Marcus' mind and he began remembering what happened.

Gina was Phil's daughter and Marcus' girlfriend. They began dating midway through their senior year in college and had been together for two years. Gina worked as a loan officer in a bank and

Marcus worked for a commercial building contractor. Neither of them was crazy about their jobs but they knew employment was important if they were going to move on to the next phase in their relationship-marriage.

Marcus and Gina were deeply in love, and it seemed that lately the idea of marriage kept coming up more and more in their conversations. He hadn't officially asked Gina-he knew her answer would be yes, but the hurdle he was facing was standing in the hospital room patting his arm.

Although Marcus got along well enough with Mrs. Pettigrove, he was convinced that Gina's father didn't like him. Their conversations were always short and direct and Phil's rough demeaner always seemed to rise to the top whenever Marcus was at their house. Gina tried to reassure him that her father was just being overprotective, but Marcus wasn't convinced.

Still, before he asked Gina to marry him, he felt compelled to have a conversation with Phil and ask his permission. In a strange way, he believed that asking for his blessing might endear him to the man. Marcus had determined that despite his anxieties, he would go by the Pettigrove's home and have the awkward conversation soon.

Just then the doctor came in and explained to Marcus his condition. He told him that he had a grade three concussion and that he needed to stay one more night for observation. He also informed him that the prognosis for total recovery was positive. Marcus forced a smile, nodded, and gave a weak "thank you."

Though Marcus' head was throbbing, everything started to come back into focus. He and Gina had gone out to dinner. Nothing fancy, but a nice Italian restaurant that had become their favorite. The parking lot was full, so they had to park in an adjacent lot.

They enjoyed their meal bypassing dessert due to full stomachs. Then they left the restaurant and walked over to their car. When they walked between the cars to Gina's side the trouble began. Two young men seemed to come out of nowhere and stepped behind them. The front of their car was against the building so their exit was blocked. Two other men were near the back of the car, so they were both trapped as well as outnumbered.

One of the men stepped up to Marcus and scowled, "Your money and your girl are going with us."

Marcus wasn't much for physical confrontations, but he tried to look strong and brave. "My money you can have, but you're not getting my girl." With that he slid Gina behind him while reaching for his wallet.

Before he had a chance to defend himself, a right fist struck him on the cheek. Gina screamed and Marcus fell against the car.

Moments later Marcus was being punched and kicked as the other three young men jumped in the crowded space and joined in. Several times Marcus tried to get to his feet but only met with another fist. Marcus fought the best he could but never landed a punch. The best he could do was roll and crawl to position himself between the men and Gina. He was knocked unconscious not knowing what was happening to Gina.

"Gina told me what happened Marcus" Mr. Pettigrove said. "Several people came by, and the guys took off. You came to the hospital in an ambulance."

"And Gina?" Marcus asked fearing what he might hear.

"They never laid a hand on her. When the crowd showed up, they ran."

Marcus gave a heavy sigh and said, "Good."

Phil pulled his chair up close to the side of the bed. "Listen Marcus. I know you and Gina want to get married. Gina's been hinting that you've been wanting to ask me for her hand." Marcus nodded afraid of what might come next.

"Let me tell you something" Mr. Pettigrove said quietly. "Any man who would stand up and defend my daughter the way you did deserves to be her husband. And I will be glad to call you my son-in-law."

Marcus' face lit up and the pain seemed to be leaving his body. "Thank you. Thank you so much."

Just then the door opened, and Gina stepped in. Seeing Marcus awake brought a beam to her face as she strode across the room to Marcus' bed. She gave Marcus a kiss on the forehead and asked, "Are you okay?"

Marcus smiled and said, "Just a little pain, kind of like when a train hits you." He avoided laughing because of his ribs.

"I was so scared!" Gina said. "I thought they were gonna kill you. Those other men showed up just in time."

"Yea, I know," Marcus added.

Gina and her father stepped back as a nurse came in and began taking his vital signs and recording them. Marcus' hands went below the blanket and were fidgeting with something at his side.

Marcus asked the nurse to move the bed so he could sit up a little. She moved it up several inches with Marcus clinching the rail. When the nurse left, Gina stepped back into her former place next to her love.

"I wanna ask you somethin' Gina" he said taking her hand in his. "And before you answer, remember, I'm a man in great pain."

Then taking his other hand out from the blanket he revealed a paper clip bent into a circle. He held up the crooked ring and asked, "Will you marry me?

Gina was completely surprised and didn't answer right away. Instead, she glanced toward her father.

With a grin, Phil nodded showing his approval.

Gina's face could hardly contain her smile. "Yes! Yes, of course I will."

She bent down but stopped just short of giving him a hug but did kiss him on his swollen lips.

Marcus winced, but then smiled. "I guess love really does hurt" he said.

Both Gina and her dad returned the smile, and the rest of the visit was spent making plans for the wedding.

-40-
DARK ANSWERS

Greg stepped inside the front door and walked into the kitchen. Danielle turned from the sink, gave him a smile, and returned his embrace. He reached around her and grabbed a French Fry. While chewing it, he asked, "Where's Mack?"

Mack was their eight-year-old son. He was both healthy and smart and was easily liked. But Mack was struggling. He had a deep and unexplainable fear of the dark. They had talked with him about it several times and tried to reason with him, but to no avail. Mack simply would not listen to logic.

On more than one occasion, Greg sat him down and explained how there was nothing in the dark that was not in the light. With that explanation, he would turn off the lights and be met with an arm around his leg and the heavy breathing of his son.

Greg and Danielle had sought council but found no concrete answers. Mack himself had been counseled with no change. Even the talk of darkness brought anxious reactions from their son. Wherever Mack was, the lights had to be on. He slept with two or three lights on and even avoided putting his head under the covers.

The couple was frustrated, confused, and carried a deep sense of hopelessness. They continually wondered if Mack would indeed grow out of it as so many had told them. They were fatigued from the conversations they were having regarding their son.

That evening, Danielle's response surprised Greg. "He's in the hammock in the back yard."

"Really?" Greg asked. "You're kidding."

"No, I'm not" she said, guiding him to the kitchen window. "Take a look."

Greg leaned forward and could see the outline of his son laying in the hammock. "Unbelievable!" Greg said shaking his head. "How did this happen?"

"Well," Danielle began. Mack brought a book home from school. It was a story of the Navajo Indians.

"The Navajo Indians?" Greg asked.

"Yes" she said. "You know the interest he's always had in the culture of the Native Americans."

Greg's mind flashed back to a vacation trip the family had taken two years ago. They were in the mid-west and were visiting an Indian town. Mack got exposed to their culture and even talked with several of the Indians. From that day on, Mack enjoyed reading books and watching movies regarding the American Indians.

Danielle continued, "Well this book he brought home had a story about a group of Navajo Indians in New Mexico. The story said that at one time the Navajo Indians were greatly afraid of the dark. When the sun went down, they retreated to their tents in fear and never came out in the dark."

Greg grabbed a few more fries and leaned against the counter as Danielle continued. "Well, one day, a wise man came into their village. He told them that God always protected them and gave them the sun to let them know of his presence. Of course, when it got dark, the people felt that God had left them, and they were filled with fear. But the wise man told them that the darkness was given by God to help them rest and that God sent a message to them to drive out their fear and to let them know that He never leaves them."

"When the day was over, God put a blanket over the sun. But to let the people know that he was still around, he put holes in the blanket. And the little lights you see in the sky are the sun coming through the holes." Danielle tipped her head to the side and smiled at her husband.

"And that's all it took? A story?" Greg asked.

"That's all it took," she said shrugging her shoulders. "Wow" Greg said. "Why didn't we find that book sooner?"

"Don't know. Don't care. All I know is that there's a little boy who doesn't seem to be afraid of the dark anymore."

"Right!" Greg said as he kissed her, hugged her, and moved toward the sliding glass door to join his son…in the dark.

-41-
TOSSING KINDNESS

Nine-year-old Colin loved his Grandpa Howard. As time drew near for a visit, his parents sensed Colin's excitement growing. On the day when they would be together Colin was almost giddy. His parents knew he would be up early and that they would be plastered with questions about what time Grandpa Howard would arrive or how close they were to leaving for his place.

Grandpa Howard was a Vietnam veteran. He had seen enough atrocities for a room full of people. Death and near-death experiences were forever etched in his mind. He had lost his wife to cancer several years ago and suffered from bouts of skin cancer himself. Yet, the old man never let the hardships of life truncate his love for people and especially his love for his only grandson.

All those who were close to him agreed that he was kindness personified. And Colin's parents were more than happy for the influence he had over their son's life. When Howard visited or when they traveled to his place Colin's parents could see a definite positive change in Colin's attitude and outlook.

They were amused when they could hear Howard's words coming from Colin's mouth as he shared with them life lessons and quips that Howard had taught him. They came to expect their son to use phrases like: "No roots, no shoots, no fruits" and "an attitude of gratitude flavors everything you do." His parents shook their heads in wonder as he taught them that, "Love is like a candle. The flame doesn't get any smaller by sharing."

They were often filled with amazement and pride as their son would break away from them to help someone lighten the load life had placed on them. He would push an elderly woman's shopping cart, hold doors open for others, and readily share a piece of candy with a child in the park. On more than one occasion he returned to their table to add a couple of quarters to the tip his parents left at a restaurant or diner.

Yes, Colin was a young man who was growing both in body and mind. And his heart was keeping pace with each of them. The size of his heart was seen one day as the family was vacationing at the beach.

On the second day of their trip a strong storm had arisen. The family was forced to stay inside until the following day. Early that morning, Colin accepted his dad's offer to go for a walk on the beach.

When the two of them reached the sand, they were amazed that the tide had washed ashore enormous amounts of starfish. As far as the eye could see, the beach was littered with the helpless creatures. With the heat from the rising sun, they were destined to dry up and die.

As they began their walk along the beach, Colin began picking up the starfish, glancing at them, then throwing them as far as he could into the surf. His father watched him for several minutes as this activity interrupted their stroll.

Finally, he asked Colin, "Son, look at all the starfish. There must be a million of them. In the big picture, do you think it makes any difference?"

Without hesitation, Colin picked up another starfish, held it before his father, and said, "It makes a difference to this one!" Then he heaved it into the foaming ocean and bent down for another one.

(Adapted from *The Star Thrower* by Loren Eiseley)

-42-

RUDENESS INTERUPTED

He didn't want to become angry. He didn't want to become a cynic. He didn't want to become a grouchy old man. But because of all his encounters lately, David felt himself slowly sliding in that direction.

It seemed like his entire week was filled with intersections of selfish, inconsiderate people who only saw themselves and what they wanted. Their focus was internal and when anyone interrupted their schedules or plans, trouble was soon to follow.

At the grocery store he met two people who deliberately cut in front of him even though his arms were full, and he'd been standing in line for several minutes. He cleared his throat thinking that they might notice him, but they each looked right through him as though he was invisible.

While driving to the mall he crossed paths with several people who drove as if they owned all three lanes. One man cut him off causing him to hit both the brakes and the horn at the same time. When he came to the light and stopped next to the man, he was shown the universal sign of discontent. "How could someone be so rude?" he thought avoiding both eye contact and confrontation.

Stopping for lunch brought him no relief. No one held a door. No one said hello. No one even looked in his direction. Even the woman at the counter acted as if he was inconveniencing her. He wasn't looking for special treatment. He just wanted to meet someone with good manners-someone who was nice-someone who would demonstrate just a fleck of kindness.

When he finally arrived home, he was quietly relieved to be alone. His wife was away at her sister's house for the weekend. Being alone meant no people and no people meant no rudeness, no selfishness, no meanness. David mused, "At least now I only have to put up with myself."

Early the next morning he was glad to be meeting with his mentor Stephen. Stephen and David had been friends for over ten years and had been meeting for breakfast, lunch, or coffee about once a week. A few minutes with Stephen and one would easily see that he was a man of wisdom and experience. He had a gentle and calming demeanor and with just a short visit one could not help but learn something from him.

When David arrived at the coffee shop, Stephen was already seated. They exchanged greetings and caught up with some of the details of each other's lives. Stephen could see the strain on David's face and sensed the trouble in his voice.

"You seem stressed this morning," he asked.

David gave a heavy sigh and asked, "Is it that obvious?"

"I'm afraid so," Stephen said.

"Well," David started, "It seems like everywhere I turn I meet an army of people who are rude, mean, and selfish. Doesn't anyone care about anybody else anymore?"

"Of course they do," Stephen said. "You just happened to run into a string of people who haven't learned to choose kindness over personal desires."

"You got that right," David said with a sigh. "Seems like everywhere I went yesterday I ran into people who had a 'Me only' attitude. They acted like they were the only people on the planet."

Stephen's head tipped to the side as he said, "Well, that's how some people are wired."

Following another small sigh, David said, "Well I met a bunch of them who need to be re-wired."

Then Stephen followed with what he so often did when they were together. He gently launched into a life lesson.

"The first thing we need to remember when we encounter *Me only* kind of people is that kindness is a choice that comes in seed form. Not everybody chooses it and not everybody nurtures it to maturity."

David nodded in understanding.

"Then we need to resist letting them decide how we're going to feel and how we're going to live. Our tendency is to match our attitude with theirs and often it is our attitude that dips down to their level."

David was silent as he understood that wisdom was being placed on the table.

Stephen continued, "Because we don't know all that other people are going through, we need to administer some EGR to them."

David's face showed his confusion.

"E.G.R. stands for *Extra Grace Required*."

This statement was followed by an understanding nod from David.

Stephen placed the palms of both hands on the table. David was used to this posture and recognized that Stephen was coming to the end of the lesson.

"When all else fails call for the faithful dog *FIDO*. We often need to handle our encounters with people like water off a duck's back. F.I.D.O. stands for Forget It and Drive On."

David gave a gentle nod letting these words sink in deeply.

Then Stephen finished with an illustration. "A man once lived next door to a dog that had the habit of barking at the full moon. Do you know how the moon responded?" Then he paused for a response.

Having no idea, David simply said, "No clue."

Stephen leaned forward for emphasis, "The moon doesn't respond. It just goes right on shining."

This was followed by a nod of understanding from David. The men finished with some small talk and emptied their booth and their coffee exiting through different doors.

David was following a man holding a to-go bag. The man walked out the door and let it go not bothering to look behind him. The door swung almost shut as David grabbed it and reversed its direction. He paused on the sidewalk and thought to himself, *E.G.R.* then looked down as if to get the attention of a dog and whispered, "Come on FIDO, let's go home."

-43-
CONNECTED HEARTS

Bill and Alice were not in the market for a dog. "Too much trouble and responsibility" they reasoned. Besides that, they agreed that a dog would tie them down, putting a cramp in their freedom. But when they attended the town's small fourth of July parade, they saw a puppy and knew that he was meant to be part of their family.

A young boy was walking in the parade with the pup draped in a sign that read, "I'm free! Take me home!" So, take him home they did.

Before they reached their home, they agreed on a name for their new pet. They didn't bother asking the young man what the puppy's name was because they knew they wanted to name him themselves. By the time they pulled into the driveway, the name *Champ* was permanently affixed to the dog and having no children of their own, he became as much a part of the family as any child would.

Champ was a brown Labrador with big paws promising a big frame. Instantly he became attached to Bill and Alice and in time grew to be a compliant and protective dog. Long walks, ball chasing, and time in the local pond all became part of Champ's resume.

Whenever a threat appeared, Champ always put himself between his *parents* and the point of danger. A doorbell, a loud noise, or a stranger in the yard, promptly brought Champ to the scene with a bark and an intimidating growl.

One spring day, as Alice was preparing their garden, two good-sized dogs wandered onto the property. They cautiously approached Alice and stood between her and the house. Alice made sure to keep her shovel between her and the dogs. One of the dogs began to bark at Alice which brought a wave of fear over her.

But her fear was relieved when Champ charged from the garage barking as he ran. Without hesitation he leapt on the larger of the two dogs and latched onto the back of his neck. The other dog joined the fight biting Champ on the shoulder and leg. It was a short but violent fight ending when both dogs decided they had had enough and scrambled away.

Champ limped over to Alice and sat down in front of her. He looked up at her as if to ask, "Are you okay?" Alice gave him a big hug and kissed him on the head. She looked at his wound and decided that a trip to the vet was in order. After an antibiotic injection and five sutures, Champ and Alice were wheeling their way back home.

But Champ was not the only thing that began to grow into Bill and Alice's life. Unbeknownst to them, cancer was growing in Bill's lungs. Six months and two rounds of chemo revealed no change. And shortly after making the decision to stop the treatments, Bill was gone.

Friends and family gathered around Alice bringing her support and comfort. But no comfort was any stronger or lasted longer than that given by Champ. He seemed to sense her sorrow and carried much of it himself. He positioned himself closer to her and often came and rested his head on her lap. Formerly he was not allowed on the couch or the bed but somehow, he seemed to know that an exception was called for. For several nights in a row, he slept with Alice and endured countless television shows on the couch by her side.

The years went by with Champ becoming a permanent fixture in Alice's life. With few exceptions, everywhere Alice went, Champ would be found by her side. So, when Alice made a quick trip to the grocery store, Champ was in his usual place in the passenger seat with his head out the window taking in the countless samples from the wind.

But moments later, life changed in a flash. Neither Champ nor Alice saw the mid-sized truck run the light and crash into Alice's door. In an instant, both driver and passenger were knocked unconscious, and Champ was thrown out the window and into the bushes.

Shortly, Alice was lifted into an ambulance and carried to a nearby hospital. She suffered from a concussion, a broken wrist, a small cut on her cheek, and several bruises. But her greatest concern was for her dog.

She was kept in the hospital overnight and was released midway through the following day. Her cousin Nancy arrived to transport her home and all Alice could think about was poor Champ. She didn't know what had happened to him but hoped and prayed that he survived and was being taken care of by someone who arrived on the scene. Alice's pain in her body was minor compared to the pain in her heart.

When Nancy pulled into the driveway she was treated to a glimpse of the relationship between her cousin and her dog. There in the center of the driveway lay Champ. When he recognized Alice in the car he rose to his feet and barked with delight. His tail was wagging wildly, and his front paws kept bouncing off the concrete.

An immediate reunion was celebrated on the front lawn with Alice sitting down and Champ climbing on her lap and licking her face. Her wounded wrist went unnoticed as Alice rubbed his belly and repeatedly kissed his head. Nancy stood in the driveway shaking her head and smiling as the two demonstrated their love, affection, and dedication toward one another. And both Alice and Champ enjoyed many more years together building special memories as only a dog and his master can.

-44-
A CONFIDENT LOVE

Ricon was a coastal town on the western edge of Puerto Rico. It boasted of bright white sand, a pounding surf, and clear turquoise water. It was a well-known destination of tourists and was full of life no matter the time of day. Eight-year-old Victor and his family had lived there his entire life, and never discussed leaving. This was their town and they loved it.

That Monday morning Victor awoke with a stretch and a yawn followed by a slight smile. His mind wandered back to the wonderful time he and his family had enjoyed over the weekend. They had been camping in the mountains and experienced a great time hiking, fishing, and sitting around a large campfire. It was not uncommon for them to enjoy such get-a-ways, and the excitement of the adventure always seemed to last a long time for Victor. His was a close-knit family and even at such a young age, Victor knew he was a blessed young man.

He heard his mother's voice in the kitchen talking with his father and knew that it was time that he slid from his bed and dressed for school.

He stumbled down the stairs and made his way to the kitchen table. As he passed his father, he received a loving pat on the back. His mom bent over, kissed the top of his head, and followed it by straightening his hair. He ate a hearty breakfast of bacon and eggs and washed it down with some orange juice.

While he ate, his mother was filling his book bag with his lunch and his books. Before he had finished his breakfast, Victor spied his buddies coming down the street and knew he had to hustle. He gulped down the rest of his juice, grabbed his backpack, received his normal kiss from his mom and hug from his dad, and trotted toward the door.

With a skip in his step, Victor joined his friends on the sidewalk and the gang headed off to school. It was an overcast day, but the boys gave it no notice. There was too much energy in the group to be bothered by such trivial things as the weather. With plenty of conversation, laughter, pushing and shoving, they arrived at the front door of the school, checked in, and made their way to their third-grade room.

Class began in the usual way. Mrs. Alexika gave the day's orders and shared a few thoughts about the upcoming history lesson. While she was speaking several of the students turned to face the window. The trees were telling them that the wind was picking up and they made a few sounds of surprise as they witnessed papers, leaves, and a large plastic trash can bounce by. Mrs. Alexika raised her voice to get their attention while at the same time silently noting the strength of the wind.

A few minutes later, the headmaster's voice was heard over the intercom. The students were instructed to move to the cafeteria quickly and quietly. Victor and his friends complied but kept their eyes on the windows as they moved toward the door. They saw more and more evidence of the storm intensifying.

In the cafeteria, the students were told to stay away from the windows and to sit quietly at the tables in the center of the room. They sat at the tables but were anything but quiet. Through the large windows they witnessed torrents of rain and bursts of wind that were new to their young eyes.

Those who were not afraid simply didn't understand what was going on around them. The lights blinked several times and then went out. With each new attack from the storm a new level of fear swept over both the students and the teachers. They could see the large windows moving as the wind continued to assault the building. They heard a *boom!* Then another *boom!* A third *boom* was louder than the other two combined. The sound was deafening and seemed to be getting closer as the storm raged. With each burst from the outside, a new and louder burst was heard from those inside. It was as if they were in the midst of a military attack.

Then a tree was thrown against the side of the building breaking three windows simultaneously. Every voice in the room screamed including those of the adults. The headmaster ordered the students under the tables, and they complied without protest or hesitation.

In their darkened state, the students' young ears could only hear what was going on outside. The increasing noise was telling them that nature was having its way and destruction lay just beyond the walls. Two more windows broke as blown items smashed into them. Fear was the universal emotion of the group.

More screams were heard as part of the roof lifted off and a deluge of water poured into the room. The water flew across the floor soaking everyone. The wind could now be felt through the large opening chilling those on the outside parameter of the huddled crowd.

Next, a wall came crashing down as the wind tore into the edifice. Many of the students were hit by the flying debris and the screams of fear were now joined by screams of pain. The missing wall allowed more of the pounding wind to attack them as they fought to escape the combination of wind, rain, and flying *missiles*.

Then the unthinkable happened. The remaining roof collapsed. Several of those near the outside of the group were immediately knocked unconscious and many more were now bleeding from the wounds they received. The dozens of students and teachers were now in a thick dark cave formed by the roof laying on top of the tables.

The hurricane raged on for another hour and then abated as quickly as it had arrived leaving a gentle rain and destruction in its wake along the entire coastal area. There was a palatable panic throughout the island as rescue workers dove into the task of helping those caught in the grip of the storm.

A large group of rescuers, neighbors, and parents raced to the building and began picking franticly through the rubble that once was the elementary school.

Fear and uncertainty gripped their hearts and minds. The concrete slab the main part of the school rested on was completely clear and a large bulge was prominent over the former cafeteria. Prayers were breathed as the people joined in to attack the roof.

The student's screams and tears were motivated by a mixture of pain and fear but went unheard by the outside ears.

Suddenly, a man digging in the center of the pile shouted, "I hear someone!" The pace of the rescuers picked up and several minutes later more voices could be heard. Trees, branches, bricks, wood, and concrete were removed as fast as humanly possible and within two hours a burst of light could be seen by those trapped below. A cheer went up from both the inside and the outside as a tunnel was dug through the rubble.

Soon, the children and adults were being helped out of the cave. The opening was slowly enlarged and now was big enough for the rescuers to enter the debris-filled room. Several of the unconscious were lifted out and immediately carried to the side for medical attention. None of the victims were killed but many had to spend extended time in the hospital.

When Victor's turn came for escape, he crawled through the opening and was lifted out by the waiting arms of his father. His dad held him close and gently hugged him as he carefully made his way toward his crying wife.

Then his dad's face burst into thankful tears as Victor looked up at him and strongly said, "Les dije que vendrias! Les dije que vendrias!"

"I told them you would come! I told them you would come!"

-45-
THE FACE OF LOVE

Adam and Joelle were a sweet young couple. They had been married for four years and had enjoyed their lives together with friends, family, and plenty of activity. Joelle was a woman who could easily be labeled beautiful both in form and face. She exercised both her brain and her body with regularity, and both were in evidence when one spent time with her. Adam was a strong handsome man. He worked hard and he played hard. He enjoyed hiking and sports and was quick to jump at the chance to be involved with either activity.

The two of them met during a church conference in a neighboring state and began dating immediately. After six months they were engaged and five months later were married. They fully enjoyed their relationship and seemed to grow closer as time marched by.

But now they sat in the doctor's office stunned. He had just told them the results of the biopsy of the small mark on Joelle's face and the slight numbness in her cheek. The words *skin cancer* and *malignant* echoed in their brains. How could this be? She had no traces of cancer in her family line and was somewhat careful about her exposure to the sun. Both she and Adam struggled to get their brains wrapped around all that Doctor Benton was telling them.

About two months earlier, Joelle noticed a small mole-like speck on her left cheek. She kept an eye on it and was diligent in keeping it clean. Then two weeks ago she thought that perhaps it had changed color and grown slightly. That was when she also felt a very slight numbness just under where the growth was. That motivated her to seek the appointment with the dermatologist.

By the time her appointment date arrived, she noticed that the corner of her mouth seemed to sag a little when she smiled. It was such a small sag that no one else would have noticed it, but Joelle did, and it brought fear to her heart like she had never experienced before. Something was definitely wrong.

"We have to do surgery as soon as possible," the Doctor said. "This is a fast-growing type of malignancy, and it lies very close to the eleventh facial nerve and two facial lymph nodes." The couple both nodded, and Joelle tried to hold back the tears birthed from fear.

Surgery was scheduled for the following week. Those seven days dragged on like never before for the couple and they were filled with prayer, conversations, and sleepless nights. Joelle found herself constantly wrestling with the question, "How could this be happening?"

The night before the surgery, Adam and Joelle enjoyed a nice meal at their favorite restaurant. They talked the entire time with Adam weaving comments about his love for her throughout their dinner. He did his best to reassure her of his love and commitment toward her and she received it gracefully and thankfully. Another night of fitful sleep followed for both of them.

Joelle and Adam were alone in the curtain drawn pre-op room. It was almost time for the surgery. He prayed a short and simple prayer over her as she lay on the gurney. Then he bent down a gave his wife a loving kiss on the lips. Their special moment was interrupted by a nurse who came in to administer some pre-op medicine. "The staff is ready, so it's time to go" she said. With that, an aide stepped in, released the brakes, and wheeled her down the hall.

Adam sat in the waiting room with his mother and father. For the most part, they engaged in small talk as they sipped their cups of coffee. They knew that the surgery was scheduled for three hours so they did their best to ignore the clock on the wall. Finally, the waiting room screen moved her initials from *In surgery* to *Finishing up*. It was at that moment that Adam felt the return of all his earlier anxiety.

Then the moment arrived. Joelle's initials came onto the screen letting them know that she was being taken to the recovery room.

Finally, Adam could see his wife. He willed his legs to walk under control as he jumped from his chair and headed through the double doors. A short trip down the corridor brought him to her room.

When he walked in, Doctor Benton was standing next to her bed. Joelle was holding a mirror and looking at her face. Adam came to the opposite side and wanted to hug her but didn't want to interrupt the doctor. He heard her ask him, "Will my mouth always be like this?" "I'm afraid so" the doctor responded. "It's because the tumor was wrapped around the nerve and had to be cut so I could remove it. We got all the tumor but had to take part of the nerve too. I'm sorry."

Joelle nodded and was silent. She picked up the mirror again and looked at her mouth as she smiled. It was twisted as her right side moved upward but the left corner stayed dormant.

Then Adam stepped even closer. His next movement and words signified nothing but love in his heart for his wife. He smiled and said, "I like it! I think it's kinda cute." Then he bent down and twisted his lips to match those of Joelle's and kissed her on the new shape of her lips. And in that moment, Joelle found peace and was relieved that their kiss still worked.

(Adapted from *Mortal Lessons: Notes on the Art of Surgery* by Richard Selzer.)

-46-
A FATHER'S PERSPECTIVE

Doug was an auto mechanic, and a really good one. And as far as anybody knew, he had always been a mechanic and seemed to be able to fix anything. He, his wife Tasha, and their ten-year-old son Jake lived in the small town of Elton just outside of Damascus, Virginia. Their home was small, but as expected, neat and well-kept.

Doug's shop was a busy one. He could be found there during the week and often on Saturdays. He had two younger men working with him and the shop was always brimming with activity. When Doug wasn't in his shop, he could be found working in the yard or spending time with Tasha and Jake. He was a mechanic and a family man in every sense of the word.

But the work in the shop eventually took its toll, and Doug found that his back began to give him increasing amounts of pain. All the lifting of heavy tools and equipment had strained his back to the point where he would come home bent over and with a noticeable limp. When he sat for any length of time, he had to rise slowly to avoid a shot of pain. He labeled this movement, "Warming up the muscles."

Doctor Helms told him that the muscles in his back had been worn out and that he needed to slow down and limit the weight he lifted as well as the position he held while doing his work. He had what was called "Activity induced muscle strain." He was told that his back would not heal unless he gave it a great deal of rest.

But resting did not come easy for Doug. His was a lifetime of work and he enjoyed being active the way some people enjoy eating. He tried to slow down but his desire for progress outweighed the resulting pain each day's end brought. He would often limp into the house and collapse in his chair for an hour or so before gingerly getting up to work his way to the dinner table.

Jake was aware of his dad's condition and limited his requests for his father to join him in some activity. He remembered and missed the days when he was younger and the two of them would shoot baskets, wrestle, or throw a ball in the front yard. Somehow his young mind realized that those who grow older and feel the effects of aging are not the only ones who struggle with it. Still, the boy yearned for time with his otherwise strong and loving father.

But Jake was not the only one who missed the active days. When Doug watched Jake shooting baskets, throwing the ball against the side of the garage, or climbing a tree, he recognized that this heart was walking outside of his body.

Tasha too felt a tug on her heart when she understood that her son was longing for his dad to join him. Her redundant comments to Doug about slowing down and being careful had their effect but it was not a lasting one. Each time Doug struggled up the steps, she would give a heavy sigh and meander down the hall to retrieve both his slippers and his pain medicine.

She also missed the feeling she got when she looked out the window to see her two men tossing a ball or playing hoops. She remembered, with fondness, how the two of them would begin moving the coffee table and the chairs in the living room to make room for a grueling wrestling match. She smiled and shook her head when she thought about how her warnings of breaking the furniture went largely unheeded.

One Saturday afternoon Pastor Knox stopped by to say hello and to check on Doug. He was very surprised to find Doug and Jake tossing a baseball in the front yard. He was very aware of Doug's condition and knew this activity wasn't recommended by the doctor.

Every time Doug threw the ball, the action sent a spark of pain down his back, and he would wince. He was able to hide the pain on his face by clinching his jaw tight and turning his head to the side. The pastor noticed it, but the results were largely unseen by Jake.

After several more throws, it was time to take a break on the porch. Tasha came out with some iced tea and a pain pill. The two men sat down, while Jake gulped his drink down and retreated to the back yard. The pastor noticed how gently Doug dropped into his chair and commented on it.

"Looks like that back of yours is hurting quite a bit."

"Yep," Doug said. "It doesn't take much to make it flair up. I'll be okay in a little while."

"Well," Pastor Knox added, "I don't think throwing a baseball is on your list of approved activities."

"Oh, it's not," Doug agreed. "But you see that boy who just jumped off the porch?"

The pastor nodded.

"That young man is growing up so fast. With children, the days are long, but the years are short. It seems like just yesterday we brought him home in a bassinette."

"I know what you mean," the pastor said. "Our son, James, headed off for college just after he learned to walk."

Both men chuckled and Doug continued.

"Well, I know my time with Jake is limited. Kids these days are pulled in so many directions and a lot of them aren't good."

"I see you've been listening to my sermons," the pastor said as he smiled.

Doug nodded and returned the smile.

"Jake will be leaving home soon too. So, I've made a painful decision." He paused to keep his emotions in check. I've chosen to have a backache today so that I won't have a heartache tomorrow."

The pastor nodded in agreement and both men smiled and enjoyed the rest of their porch time and tea.

-47-
LARGE RESOURCES

"You'll be fine!" Eli's mother said as she pulled into the school drop-off area. "Just do the best you can and try to be nice to everybody." Eli nodded and headed to the front door of Cranmer Middle School. The first day of school is always hard but it's notably harder when you're *the new kid.*

Eli and his family had recently moved to Cranmer from Grand Rapids, Michigan. A change in jobs had brought them to the small town, just outside of Raleigh, North Carolina. They arrived only a week before the start of school and had little time to settle in. A quick tour of the town and school and Eli was off to start his seventh-grade year.

Eli was an average student with a less-than-average interest in school. Most would label him an introvert although he did have a close-knit set of friends he had left behind up north. When it came to this new venture in Cranmer, he had a *mind your own business and just get through it* kind of attitude.

It didn't take long before most of the students were aware of Eli's *newness.* After second period, he stopped at his locker to exchange books. As soon as he opened the locker door, he felt it slam shut just missing his fingers. The closed door revealed two boys laughing and bouncing down the hall. One of them looked over his shoulder and yelled, "Welcome to Cranmer Yank!"

"So, this is how they do things in North Carolina," Eli thought as he took a deep breath and turned the combination dial to re-open his locker. "So much for southern hospitality."

Things in the cafeteria went as expected. He worked his way through the line choosing items that looked better than they tasted. He was largely left alone but could feel the stares as he walked with his tray and sat down. A couple of girls walked by his table and smiled as they said "Hey," but they kept on walking. A slight smile came to Eli's face as he silently quipped, "I thought they'd never leave."

The next day brought more of the same. Eli spent most of the day with his head down and his feet moving. His locker wasn't slammed shut but the same two boys knocked his books out of his hands in the crowded hall. All the students simply walked past him as he stooped to gather his books and papers.

That's when he met Howard. Howard was a tall thin kid with thick glasses and a broad smile. When Eli stood up, Howard was standing in front of him.

"I'm Howard," he said as he extended his hand in a gesture of friendship.

Eli shook his hand and simply said, "Hi! I'm Eli."

"I see you've met the school idiots," he said turning his head in the boys' direction.

"Yeah, real nice guys," Eli answered. "I guess every school has a couple of them."

Howard held up three fingers and said, "Actually, there's three of 'em. Don't worry about it, I got your back."

Eli nodded and thought, "Yeah right! What are you gonna do, kill 'em with kindness?"

"You're in Myre's English class, right?" Howard said-more of a statement than a question.

"Yeah," was all that the Eli offered.

"I'm in that class too. Mr. Myre's a good guy. He's kinda weird, but he's alright."

Eli only answered with a nod.

After class, the two boys walked to the cafeteria and sat together. Eli began to open up a bit and also learned a great deal about Howard. Halfway through lunch a boy named James joined them and Eli thought to himself, "Maybe this won't be so bad after all."

Over the next two months, Eli learned to endure the comments and inconveniences of what he secretly called "The Bully Boys."

Books on the floor, bumps in the hall, and names followed by laughter all became part of what he expected from these young men.

But a curiosity began to settle over Eli's mind. Secretly he wondered why Howard never had to go through what Eli did. Eli thought that gangly Howard seemed to be a better target than himself. But he was largely ignored by this group of guys who felt that they were bigger when they made others feel small.

Finally, one day, during lunch, Eli posed the question to Howard. "Hey H, how come the idiot brigade never picks on you? How come they leave you alone?"

Howard grinned and said, "I have a secret weapon."

Eli leaned forward and asked, "What is it?"

Howard smiled and answered, "If I told you, it wouldn't be a secret."

"I thought that's what you'd say," Eli said shaking his head.

"Listen" Howard told him, "Come by my house on Saturday and I'll show it to you."

The conversation ended but Eli's mind was flooded with possibilities. A gun, a knife, poison? He even fought to resist the idea that Howard somehow was a Ninja Warrior.

Saturday couldn't come fast enough. When he felt that it was late enough in the morning to avoid infringement, he raced over to Howard's house. He found Howard in the garage finishing the repairs on a home-made birdhouse.

Conversation was brief before Eli brought up the subject of Howard's secret weapon. Howard moved toward the door and motioned for Eli to follow.

The two boys entered the house and made their way to the kitchen. Eli's eyes widened as he caught sight of Howard's secret weapon. Seated at the table, hovering over a plate of pancakes, was one of the largest young men Eli had ever seen.

"This is my brother, William" he said patting the man on the back. "He's home for the weekend. He's a middle linebacker for Louisburg College. They have a bye this week, so he was able to come home. William, this is my buddy, Eli."

William put down his fork and stood up. He extended his hand to Eli and said, "How ya doin'?"

"Doin' fine" was all that Eli could get out.

"Good" was all that William offered as he sat back down and went back to work on his plate.

"Let's go outside" Howard said as he led Eli out the back door.

The two boys sat on some folding chairs under the shade of a large maple tree.

Finally, Eli broke the silence, "Man he's big!"

"Strong too!" Howard answered.

Eli smiled and said, "If he was my weapon, it wouldn't be a secret for long."

Howard returned the smile and shared a story. "Those guys used to pick on me like they do you. But one day, last year, William and I were getting lunch in the deli in town. William was in the men's room when two of those guys walked in. They came over to me at the table and made a few of their stupid remarks. One of them was about to pick up my sandwich and take a bite. They never saw William behind them." Howard grinned as he relived the episode.

"William didn't say a word. He just grabbed each of them by the back of their hair and pushed them out the door. I went out behind them, but he was talking so low and so close to them that I couldn't tell what he was saying. He had them both against the store window and they looked like two scared bunnies. I'm not sure what he said, but all I know is that when they left, they took their bullying with them."

"Wow!" was all that Eli said.

Monday morning at school ushered in a different world for Eli. The gang of three went passed him several times and never even looked at him. There were no more comments, his books remained in his hands, and the need to dodge a shoulder was gone. Eli wasn't sure, but somehow knew, that over the weekend, the boys experienced another encounter with William.

And looking back, Eli recalls that his last encounter was the final one he experienced during his entire academic career. He was thankful that he now felt safe. He was thankful for his friend Howard, but he was most thankful for his new *secret weapon*. And as Eli grew and by natural default, he became a rabid fan of the Louisburg College Hurricanes.

-48-
SMALL BLESSINGS

Paul was highly discouraged and felt himself sliding into a deep depression. He was normally an upbeat person, with a quick wit and a ready smile. But life had taken a turn on him that he was neither expecting nor prepared for and it was sending him into an emotional downward spiral.

During the previous two months his mother passed away after a long battle with leukemia. He also suffered through a virus that required an overnight stay in the hospital. In the last two weeks, his car suffered from a hit and run accident, several of his appliances in his home needed repair, he lost his wallet, and his girlfriend of over six months decided to move on.

His job was no help with his mental condition. Paul was a fire-fighter in Hamilton, a good size town in rural Tennessee. He had served in Hamilton for over fifteen years and had seen more than his share of destruction and devastation. He was trained to disen-gaged from what he was exposed to but lately the struggle became harder. Somehow the difficulties others were experiencing was pen-etrating his outer shell and his heart was enveloped in their pain.

One night, during his shift at the station, Paul went to bed early. He hadn't been resting well and felt his energy ebbing faster as the day went on. He had been asleep for only two hours when the sta-tion alarm rang out. In just minutes he had joined his co-workers and they were mounting the ladder truck and speeding to the other side of town.

On arrival they found a two-story residence largely engulfed in flames. The family had all managed to escape but there was little hope in saving their home. Other members of the team were pulling up and the group quickly circled around the captain who barked out orders. The men scrambled to their assignments and did their best to beat back the flames. But each man knew that their job at this point was to contain the fire as best they could to prevent it from damaging the adjacent homes. They all knew that what the fire didn't destroy, the smoke and water would.

Paul and his crew worked diligently for over four hours. And he did his best to resist looking at the husband and wife who had lost everything but each other and their daughter. But even as he tried to resist the urge, his eyes and heart kept finding the couple and although he was busy working, the ache they felt tugged at his heart strings. For Paul it was just another dunking in the growing pool of despair.

Paul got back to the station early the next morning. He downed a quart of electrolyte juice and slumped up the stairs. He was beyond the point of exhaustion and collapsed on the bed. And then the tears came. All the frustration and disappointment of the last two months came pouring onto his pillow and he wept uncontrollably.

It wasn't that Paul didn't have faith. He was quite firm in his faith in God. He read his Bible regularly, prayed often, and attended church on Sundays when not on duty. He had always had a sense of God's very presence even during some of the most dangerous calls. But lately he felt that God was so far away. The nearness that he had felt had dried up and the issues of life had taken its place.

Between sobs Paul cried aloud,

"God where are you? I feel so alone! Why can't you make yourself known? Why can't I feel your presence? Can't you just give me a sign that you're still here?

With those last words he drifted off into a deep sleep.

Early the next morning two others joined Paul as they returned to last night's scene. Their job was to tour the burned house and look for signs of smoldering wood. They were each armed with pokers as well as fire extinguishers.

When they arrived and got out of the truck, the other two men went in the front while Paul circled around back. Close to the backdoor he saw a maple tree with the side facing the house completely scorched. Unimpressed, he went around the tree to enter the back door. As he passed the tree he looked down and noticed a dead bird lying in a nest on the ground. The wings were extended, the feathers were almost completely burned off, and the stiffness of death had settled over the little creature.

Paul paused over the animal while thinking, "Is this the sign Lord? Is this the way you're telling me you're near?" Then with a heavy sigh and a shrug he stepped over the debris and entered the back of the house.

After the men had finished their tour and were satisfied the fire was out, they walked out the back door. Paul was behind the other two and by chance looked down at the dead bird. With a mild shake of his head and without thinking about it, he nudged the bird over with his poker. And that is when he saw the three little birds under the chest of their mother. The little ones came to life stretching their necks and opening their tiny beaks.

Paul bent down while taking off his helmet. Seconds later he had scooped all three birds up and was heading toward the truck to join the other two men.   When he got to the vehicle, he slid into the back seat cradling his cap on his lap. One of the men noticed his hat and asked "Whatcha got there Paul?" Feeling life returning to his heart, Paul smiled and simply said, "A gift from an old friend."

He took the three young ones home, nursed them to maturity and set them free in his own back yard. The entire time, he felt the heaviness of life gradually leaving him while being replaced by the presence of the Lord he had always enjoyed.

-49-
KINDNESS HAS A NAME

Mark was eager to start his seminary education. He had graduated from college with honors and felt a call into the ministry early in his senior year. Due to financial difficulties, he spent his first year after college working for a painter and preaching at a small church in his hometown. It took some time but eventually he saved enough money to pay for his first three semesters of seminary.

When he arrived on campus he immediately felt at home. The students were friendly and engaging and the professors were highly knowledgeable and readily available.

Mark dove into his studies as he had done during his college career. He was well prepared for each class, and it was clear that he was enjoying the entire seminary experience.

His favorite class was Dr. Freed's *Studies in Systematic Theology.* Dr. Freed had a way of communicating that made the material easy to understand and left the students hungry for more.

On several occasions Mark sat with Dr. Freed over a cup of coffee in *Bean There* coffee shop on the edge of campus. Dr. Freed was always encouraging and carried with him a wealth of knowledge regarding pastoral life. And Mark soaked up all he had to say like a sponge.

Dr. Freed's class carried with it thirteen unannounced quizzes, two of which the students had the option of dropping. Although they were labeled *quizzes*, they usually took over thirty minutes to complete and required serious time in preparation. The quizzes comprised thirty percent of the class grade, so it was important to do well in this area.

Midway through the semester, Mark didn't have one quiz that he felt he needed to drop. He was highly motivated to do well in the class and it was reflected in his quiz grades.

Just after Thanksgiving break, another surprise quiz came out of the professor's briefcase. Just like so many others, Mark breezed through it. Then he got to the last question, "What is the first name of the woman who cleans this building?" This question caught all the students by surprise.

Mark had seen the cleaning woman several times. She was short, with short hair, and seemed to be in her mid-fifties. But how could he be expected to know her name? He handed in his paper leaving the last question blank. As the students began to leave the room, one of them asked if the last question would count toward their quiz grade.

"Absolutely" said Dr. Freed. "As you move into the pastorate, you will meet many people. Every single one of them is significant. And their names are the most valuable thing they own. They deserve your attention and respect, even if all you do is smile, call their name, and say 'Hello.'"

The very next day, Mark made a special trip to Gladstone Hall. He climbed the steps and immediately found the lady busily sweeping the floor. He got her attention and handed her a gift card for coffee. They talked for a few minutes and then he walked away after learning that her name was Regina.

It was a lesson Mark would never forget. And for the rest of his seminary career, he made sure to greet Regina by name whenever he found himself in Gladstone Hall.

-50-
THE CHOICE OF KINDNESS

Walt was eighty years old and the picture of encouragement. When it was raining his response was, "Best weather in town!" When someone asked, "How are you doing?" he would answer, "Great and getting better!" That's just he way Walt lived. That's the attitude he carried no matter the weather or circumstances.

And as far as anyone knew, Walt had always been this way. So, it was no surprise that when he was asked about his hip surgery that he responded, "Piece of cake. I slept through the entire operation." He once quipped, "The best part about becoming so forgetful that you keep meeting new friends." It was these types of responses and comments that always brought a smile and endeared him to friends and family.

Those who were close to him saw him as a *breath of fresh air*. They knew he had his moments of struggle, but also knew his positive attitude and eagerness to encourage others offset the difficult days.

And his life's history did include some very difficult days. Fifteen years ago, he lost his wife and best friend Dee to cancer. He struggled through a term in the Korean war. His house was robbed, and he was hospitalized after totaling his car. His hands were bent from arthritis, and he often suffered with lower back pain.

Still, none of these issues ruled over his life. He understood that both sadness and joy are emotions, and everyone has a choice which one they will embrace. It was quite obvious to everyone who met him, that he most often chose joy.

One day Daniel, who claimed that he was Grandpa Walt's favorite, came for a visit. Daniel was a senior in high school and always enjoyed the quick trips his family made to Walt's house. He loved the stories his grandpa told and often tucked away for later use the jokes the old man shared.

When he arrived, Grandpa met him with a hearty hug, a firm pat on the back and his usual grin.

"How ya doin'?" Walt asked.

"I'm doin' great!" Dan said. "One more month and I'll graduate. Then I'm heading off to Milton for college."

"So, you've decided to go to Milton hunh?"

"Yep! They've got a great engineering department and I think it will be a really good fit for me."

"Well then, go Tigers!" the old man said. "Milton is a good school and I'm sure you'll teach them a thing or two!"

"Yeah right, maybe even three," Daniel said with a chuckle.

The two of them strolled through the back yard while Walt pointed out some of the beautiful flowers that were beginning to bloom. When they went back inside Walt headed for the fridge to begin preparing their lunch.

The conversation continued over their sandwiches and sodas with Dan sharing the latest news from the family and his buddies at school. Walt had plenty of questions for the young man ensuring that there were no gaps in the conversation.

An hour later, it was time for Daniel to return home. As they began their good-byes, his grandfather reached into a side table drawer and pulled out a small gift bag. Handing it to his grandson, he smiled and said, "I've been wanting to give you this for a while. I know it'll be the best graduation gift you get, and I didn't want it to be overshadowed by the other junk people give you."

"Right!" Dan said with a smile.

He opened the bag and pulled out a blue hooded sweatshirt bearing the name and logo of Milton University.

"Wow!" Daniel exclaimed. He gave his grandfather a hug and added, "This is awesome! Thank you so much!"

He put the gift back in the bag and said, "Well, I gotta get going. I'll call you this week."

"Sure thing!" the old man returned.

Daniel grabbed the doorknob and was ready to open the door when he turned to face his grandfather.

"Grandpa, I've got a question for you."

"Fire away!" Walt said smiling.

"I've always wondered. Have you always been so upbeat and encouraging?"

"I dunno" he said. "We're all a product of our past, and overall, I'd say I've been a very blessed man."

Daniel nodded and said, "Yeah, I've been blessed too. But you always lift people up. Have you always been that way?"

"You got a second?" Walt said waving his hand toward the couch while moving in that direction.

Without a word, Daniel sat down next to the old man.

"It's been a long time since I've shared this with anyone," he said with a hint of a reflective grin. "When I was a freshman in college, I became part of a community service group that the Chaplain set up. We were called 'The Apex Team.' There were about twenty of us in the group and we would go out into the community and lend a hand wherever it was needed." A smile began to form on Walt's face as the memory began to materialize.

"Sometimes we would rake leaves or shovel snow. Other times we would do some painting or gardening. Once, we built a shed in a lady's back yard. We had a good time, and the group began to get closer as we did more and more projects."

Daniel's nod and lean showed he was locked into the story.

"Well, there was a freshman girl that began to come to our group. Her name was Maureen. She was a big girl and couldn't do a lot of the things we were involved in. Most times she just brought us cokes and wandered around."

"We had a couple of projects that we were doing, and I noticed that Maureen missed both. It wasn't a big deal, and nobody paid much attention to it."

"And then one afternoon I was in the bookstore, and I ran into Maureen. I said something like, 'Hey Maureen! We've been missin' you at Apex.' I'm not sure what she said, and I didn't give it much thought."

"Then a couple of days later, I was in the cafeteria with a couple of my buddies. Maureen came by with an empty tray and stopped at the end of the table. I'll never forget what she said, 'Hey Walt. You'll never know how good it made me feel to know that you missed me at Apex.' Then she just turned and walked away. But let me tell you something. She left but her words stayed."

Daniel nodded and gave a slight smile.

"It was then that I learned three things about encouragement. One-everyone needs encouragement. Two-everyone can be an encourager. And three-it doesn't take much to encourage someone and change their day."

"That's a great story Grandpa," the young man added.

Putting his hand on Dan's knee, Walt continued. "Wait, there's more. While doing my homework for an English class, I came across a quote from Maya Angelou that I've never forgotten. 'People will forget what you said, people will forget what you did, but people will never forget how you made them feel.' That statement became locked in my brain."

"The next day, I was at the gym, and I walked by one of the coach's offices. He had a quote on his door by William Arthur Ward. It said, 'Flatter me, and I may not believe you. Criticize me, and I may not like you. Ignore me, and I may not forgive you. Encourage me, and I will never forget you.'"

"I copied that quote and put it near my desk in my dorm next to the quote from Maya Angelou and those two quotes have pushed me forward ever since."

"Makes perfect sense," Daniel said standing up. Walt stood up and was immediately embraced by Dan.

"Thanks Grandpa! Thanks for everything!"

Walt smiled and said, "You make it easy."

Three months later, Daniel was on the campus of Milton University. His grandfather's influence was clearly seen in his dorm. Next to his desk, taped to the wall were both quotes Walt had given him. And like his grandfather, Daniel developed the life-long habit of encouraging others.

-51-
THE PACE OF KINDNESS

It was Thursday morning, May 6th, 1954, and Chris Chataway pressed himself up in bed. He stretched and yawned then slipped out of the covers and stretched again. This wasn't just any Thursday. This was the day he would do his best to help his good friend Roger Bannister accomplish a dream. Roger was staged to attempt to break the four-minute mile barrier, a feat the experts said was not only impossible, but life threatening.

Chris had a strong history of running. While at Magdalen College in Oxford, he set several long-distance records and won most of his races. He was better at the longer distances, but when Roger proposed his plan, Chris was quick to jump in.

He stood by the window looking down at the street and spent a few moments watching the town come to life. After getting dressed, he grabbed the bag holding his running gear, slipped on a jacket, and made his way down the stairs.

Chris stopped by the corner shop for his pre-meet meal. He was a regular there and was greeted warmly by the manager and several of the patrons. Many of them knew of the day's events and wished him well.

It would be a couple of hours before he ran, so Chris didn't hesitate in indulging in a heavy meal. Eggs, ham, and toast being washed down by a couple of mugs of coffee were his favorites and he took his time enjoying his breakfast.

The day was overcast and a bit chilly with a breeze beginning to blow-not ideal weather for such a great attempt. But the excitement of the race brought a ray of sunshine into his day, and he wound his way the six blocks to the Iffley oval.

Roger and Chris were great friends and training partners. Though both had graduated college, they continued to run for the Oxford track club. Roger was in medical school while Chris held an executive position with Guinness Brewery.

Roger was already in the locker room when Chris walked in. They greeted each other warmly and chatted for a few minutes while Chris got dressed. Shortly, Chris Brasher entered. Brasher was to be part of the running plan as well and the three men spent some time sharing bits and pieces of their lives. Roger had some misgivings about the conditions for a world record attempt but both Chris' put his doubts to rest.

As the time for warming up drew near, they discussed the simple strategy they hoped would carry Roger to his goal. Chis Brasher was to set the pace. The first two laps were to be under world record pace. Then Brasher would step off and Chataway would take the lead for the next lap keeping the pace strong. After three quarters, Chris Chataway would slip aside, and Roger would fight for the finish line.

The men warmed up together stretching and covering a couple of laps while other events were enjoyed by the growing crowd. The conversation was light but as the time for the race drew near, their voices grew quiet, and their focus became evident.

The men marched together to the starting line, joining five other runners. As their names were announced, the crowd roared to life. There was not a soul in the stadium who didn't know what was about to be attempted and everyone was anxious about the possibility of witnessing history being made.

Roger gave quick final instructions to his two friends. Turning to Brasher he said, "Remember, fast two!" Then he turned to Chataway, gently popped him in the chest with a clenched fist, and said, "Fast three!" The faces of the two men showed determination as they nodded in affirmation. The three shook hands and waited for instructions from the starter.

When the gun went off, Chris Brasher shot to the lead as expected. Chris Chataway was right behind him and held to his heels. Bannister held his position a few feet behind Chataway. The first lap was fast and completed in 57.5, right on pace.

Brasher continued to hold the lead knowing that the second lap would be his last. And Roger stayed right behind both men as they pounded the cinders together. The half mile was completed in 1:58.2. The pace was as strong as were the men.

After crossing the line at the half-way mark, Chris Brasher slid to the side and cruised to a stop. Following the plan, Chris Chataway took the lead and continued to pour on the speed with Roger right behind. Such a fast pace caused the men's lungs to begin to burn but slowing down never entered their minds.

Chataway crossed the line in 3:00.5 and feeling very strong, he continued to lead around the turn. Just before the final turn, Chataway moved over to lane two as Bannister slipped ahead and pressed for the tape.

But instead of slowing down and exiting the race, Chris Chataway continued to run. He stayed close behind Bannister yelling and cheer him on. Roger's lungs were on fire, and he felt like he was carrying a mountain of weight. The crowd, sensing the impossible was within reach, brought their cheers to a deafening level.

When Bannister crossed the line, he collapsed on the infield grass. Seconds later Chataway and Brasher joined him, and the three men lay on the turf heaving for gulps of air. Numbness filled their bodies as they waited for the results to be announced.

The crowd was hushed as the speakers called out the time. Neither men heard the complete time because as the announcer said the word three, the stands erupted with cheers. The men and the fans understood that for the first time in history, the four-minute mile had been eclipsed. They later learned that Roger Bannister's time was 3:59.4.

A valuable lesson was also learned that day by Chris Chataway. He learned that when you help someone reach their goal, there are benefits that come your way as well. Chataway finished with his all-time best of 4:01.2.

After Roger did what so many others said was impossible, the four-minute mile was eclipsed again by Australian runner John Landy. And although Roger Bannister's record was broken just thirty days later, his friendship with Chris Chataway and Chris Brasher lasted a lifetime.

-52-
LOVE'S SUPPORT

Nate looked up from his desk and saw Mr. Arnold open his office door and point at him. He waved his hand toward Nate ordering him in. The grave look on the man's face signaled that whatever was about to happen, it was not going to be good.

Nate entered the office and was not invited to sit down. Mr. Arnold got right to the point. "Nate, you've done a good job here and we are grateful for your work. But we've had a strong down-turn in the business and I'm afraid we're going to have to let you go today."

Explaining the difficulty of the times and with an apology, he handed Nate a slip of paper putting in written form what he just conveyed. Along with that, he gave him his last paycheck finalizing Nate's departure.

Nate was shocked. He never saw it coming. He knew things were tight but never realized how desperate they had become. His work seemed to be going along as it had been for the last three years. He was covering his responsibilities with the usual speed and accuracy he had been known for. Now this?

The New England winter wind bit deeply into Nate's neck as he hustled his way home. How was he going to tell his wife Sophia that he had lost his job? The fact that he was let go due to the company's financial difficulties did little to ease his disappointment. "What will I do? How will we live?" he thought as another blast of air pushed him forward.

Nate and Sophia had been married for eight years, and she was the love of his life. He called her his "Dove" and could think of no one he'd rather spend his life with. She was always encouraging and supportive of everything he did and every idea that lodged in his mind.

"I know she will be so disappointed," he thought. "How am I going to tell her?" Nate's mind flashed to the couple's two children. He was a highly responsible man and saw his role as a father as *his business on earth.*

So many thoughts wrestled for dominance in his mind as he trudged homeward. He thought of his connections with friends and family. He thought of several jobs he had had and wondered if there were some possibilities there. He wondered where they would go if they had to move.

When Nate entered the house his daughter Una yelled, "Daddy's home!" and raced to her father's arms. He swept her up and gave her an all-embracing hug. Then he carried her to the kitchen where Sophia was preparing dinner and sliding bits of food to their one-year-old son in his highchair. Sophia was surprised to see him and said, "You're home a little early. Is everything okay?"

Nate put Una down and she raced back to her dolls in the other room. He then slid over to Julian and kissed him on the head and turned to his wife who was now facing him. "Not really," he said as he sat down at the table and lowered his head. "They let me go today."

Sophia sat down at the table next to him and put her hand on his forearm. "What happened?"

Nate gave a heavy sigh, "Nothing really. Old man Arnold just called me in and said they're down-sizing and I have to go."

Sophia was silent for several moments as she tried to take it all in. Then she slid closer to him and smiled. "Well, now you can write your book."

He gave her a puzzled look, "My book?"

"Yes," she said. "The one you keep telling me about. Now you have time to sit down and write it."

Nate had always loved to write. It awakened in him something that the responsibilities of life forced to dormancy. He immediately thought of a book he had written before they were wed. It was called *Fanshawe.* He self-published it and was very disappointed in its receptance. The disappointment had sidelined his writing career and forced him to move it into the hobby category. He had written several articles for magazines with moderate results, but to rely on literary success for his livelihood? The idea was more than Nate could grasp.

Turning his head to the side he said, "I would love to write my book. But what will we live on while I'm busy putting pen to paper?"

Sophia grinned widely. She patted him on the back and said, "Come with me." She led him into another room and opened a closet door. Reaching inside, she pulled down a small cardboard box. She lifted the lid exposing a hoard of cash.

Where in the world did you get all this?" the surprised man asked.

"Well, every week, I've been saving a little from what you've been bringing home from the custom house. I think we've got enough here to last us several months while you're busy writing your masterpiece."

Nate was stunned and stood silent for several moments. Then a grin emerged from his face. He leaned over, embraced his wife, and kissed her on the lips. He drew her even closer and whispered, "I have married an amazing woman!"

Sophia smiled and said, "And I have married a man who is wise enough to know that!"

They both gave a chuckle as they wandered back to the kitchen.

Shortly after dinner, Nate and Sophia put the children to bed. Then, fueled with the support of his wife, and renewed enthusiasm for his passion, Nate hunkered down in an overstuffed chair and began putting on paper the story he'd been carrying in his mind.

The more he wrote, the more he found his energies and excitement building. The next day Sophia arranged the living room so that Nate had his own space to do his work. She shielded him from too much interference from the children and sat patiently when he would read different sections of his manuscript.

Nate's book started out as a short story but quickly evolved into a large novel. The title as well as the storyline changed several times as he poured himself into his work often writing and re-writing entire chapters in a single sitting.

Finally, after several months of intense but enjoyable work, Nate's project was complete. He re-read the book making a few minor changes and then the entire family made the long-awaited trip to the post office. They paid the post man and with a heavy sigh turned the book over to him to be delivered to his friend and publisher for his evaluation and input.

When they left the post office Nate felt one hundred pounds lighter and Sophia couldn't stop grinning. They stopped on the way home for a celebratory dish of ice cream in the local shop. With their taste buds satisfied, they meandered their way back home.

Three weeks later a letter arrived from the publishing company. Accolades for the book as well as a contract were enclosed. And thus, was borne the novel we have today known as *The Scarlet Letter* by Nathaniel Hawthorne-a book that emerged when a downturn at work was countered by an up-turn at home.

ABOUT THE AUTHOR
DR. STEVEN A. JIRGAL

Dr. Jirgal is a 1980 graduate of Gettysburg College where he became a four-time conference champion, All-American, and inductee to the Middle Atlantic Conferecnce *All Century Team* in the pole vault. He holds an undergraduate degree in health education and physical education. Following graduation, he taught on the high school and college level while coaching football and track in both venues. He holds masters degrees in health education, sports medicine, and divinity, as well as a doctorate in ministry.

He has been the director of Sports Medicine at Wingate University, area director for the Fellowship of Christian Athletes and has served on the staff of Hickory Grove Baptist Church in Charlotte, NC, as well as leading Lakeview Baptist Church, in Monroe, NC and Anderson Grove Baptist Church as the Senior Pastor. He presently serves as the "Pastor to the Pastors" at Lee Park Church. He has served on the local board of directors for the Fellowship of Christian Athletes, the board of trustees at New Orleans Baptist Seminary and the ministerial board of Wingate University. He currently serves on the board of directors for The Carolina Study Center, and Fathers in Touch ministry.

Dr. Jirgal is the founder and director of *The Jirgal Leadership Institute* where he strives to equip people for success in leadership roles. He and his wife Pam have three children, Joshua, Caleb, and Sarah. They reside in Monroe, NC.

OTHER BOOKS BY DR. JIRGAL
(DESCRIPTIONS TO BE FOUND ON THE JIRGAL
LEADERSHIP WEBSITE AT JIRGALLEADERSHIP.COM)

The Path of a Champion
Dying to Live
Life Points
Laws to Live By
Principles of Wholeness
Running a Clean Race
Encounters with the Christ
The Going to Bed Book
Intentional Steps
52 Words
Mining the Mind of King Solomon
From the Pages of Qoheleth
Life in the Pearl
Christmas Stories from the Heart